SIXTY MILLION JOBS

BY

Henry A. Wallace

1945

REYNAL AND HITCHCOCK

SIMON AND SCHUSTER

All Mr. Wallace's royalties from this book are to be applied to the promotion and encouragement of scientific research and literary and educational activities in the field of economics.

ABOUT THE APPEARANCE OF BOOKS IN WARTIME

A ruling by the War Production Board has curtailed the use of paper by book publishers.

In line with this ruling and in order to conserve materials and manpower, we are co-operating by:

1. Using lighter-weight paper which reduces the bulk of our books substantially.
2. Printing books with smaller margins and with more words to each page. Result: fewer pages per book.

Slimmer and smaller books save paper and plate metal and labor. We are sure that readers will understand the publishers' desire to co-operate as fully as possible with the objectives of the War Production Board and our government.

MANUFACTURED IN THE UNITED STATES OF AMERICA
BY AMERICAN BOOK–STRATFORD PRESS, INC., NEW YORK

55

TABLE OF CONTENTS

I wish to acknowledge my indebtedness to many good friends, both in and out of Government, for their hearty and splendid co-operation in the preparation of this book. It has been my good fortune during the past thirteen years of official life in Washington to contact the minds and share the aspirations of many thoughtful men and women in the various Government agencies and in business, labor, and agricultural groups who are thoroughly devoted to the common good. I want here to express my appreciation to all of them for the encouragement they give to this country's faith in the wisdom of co-operating for the general welfare.

H. A. W.

PART ONE

The People's Peace

I

The Climate of Full Employment
and Peace

THE GOAL

I N THIS BOOK I use the total of 60 million jobs as synony-
mous with the peacetime requirements of full employment. But to argue as I do that this nation can provide
continuous full employment within the framework of our
free-enterprise system imposes a responsibility which al-
lows for no quibbling or demagoguery over facts and figures—or over synonyms and symbols.

The goal is full employment with a 200-billion-dollar
national production. We may well find, after the postwar
reconversion period, that 59 million jobs will provide us
with full employment—or that we must have 61 million
jobs to provide work for everyone who wants or needs
work. Perhaps in ten years or so, technological improvements and our ever-increasing efficiency will make it possible for us to produce 200 billion dollars' worth of goods
and services with only 55 million people at work—and with
a distribution of wages that will leave no family and no
individual beyond the benefits of this abundant national
production. If so, then we are so much healthier a nation.

3

Meanwhile, however, I think we should keep 60 million jobs as the symbol, if not the arithmetically exact synonym, of the full employment we *can* have—the full employment we *must* have to safeguard our unlimited future as a free people against the enemies of our freedom in our own homeland.

I believe that we can attain this goal without a Planned Economy, without disastrous inflation, and without an unbalanced budget that will endanger our national credit. I shall define my terms, calculate the costs, weigh the alternatives, and offer a bill of particulars. I shall not be content with a recital of the advantages of full employment, but shall give the chapter and verse of policy-making and budget-making necessary to achieve the goal.

But our full employment, just as our peace, needs the proper climate in which to thrive. We can have neither continuous full employment nor continuous peace unless we rid ourselves of the twin evils of disunity and defeatism.

THE CLIMATE OF UNITY

To end disunity—or to put it more realistically, perhaps, to keep disunity at a minimum—demands that we do some real thinking about social tensions. To get and keep full employment calls for all the energies and purposefulness of the whole nation. Enterprise which creates jobs is born of human hope and aspiration. It is the hope of the individual, his vision and courage, which makes job-creating enterprise possible. A threat against such hope is a threat against all enterprise and against our limitless opportunities. The loss of hope withers the people's energies, their

4

enterprise, their ambitions. It is absolutely essential, therefore, that we squarely face the problem of racial and religious discrimination and propaganda-bred hatred.

Social tensions, few or many, would be intolerable in our national life for any reason. But when 13 million of our people are Negroes, 23 million are Catholics, and 5 million are Jews—a total equal to about one third of our population—the existence of social tensions must be faced with boldness and courage. If America is to attain full employment and lasting peace at home, it cannot afford the social chaos of racial and religious discrimination.

Nazi barbarism began with these same racial and religious prejudices and hatred. And in their fanaticism, the Nazi terrorists even denied Christ and destroyed Christian morality as a force for unity among the peoples of the earth. It is quite clear that any organized group which would seek, through propaganda-inspired race and religious prejudice and hatred, to divide the people is guilty of the worst kind of fraud and crime against man and society.

We have learned—and we have paid for that knowledge in life and treasure—that whosoever willfully harms any part of society irreparably damages all of it. We have remedy in law against commercial fraud. Surely, racial and religious intolerance fostered by organized groups, using propaganda channels, represents nothing more nor less than social fraud—a crime against society. I firmly believe, therefore, that Congress should enact a legal remedy making such social crimes punishable—with due protection, of course, for our civil liberties.

THE CLIMATE OF PEACE

Just as lasting peace at home cannot thrive in a climate of social tensions, so can there be no lasting peace in the world if our relations with foreign countries are founded on prejudice, ignorance, and suspicion. There can be no question as to the necessity of full participation with the United Nations in helping other countries help themselves toward better living standards, for I believe that this good neighborliness spreads benefits both ways. And I want here to emphasize the necessity of avoiding and removing the defeatist tensions in international relations that are caused by constantly expecting the other fellow to take a poke at us. I have in mind particularly at this juncture our attitude toward Russia.

There is altogether too much irresponsible defeatist talk about the possibility of war with Russia. In my opinion, such talk, at a time when the blood of our boys shed on the fields of Europe has scarcely dried, is criminal. There are certain people—and they are the rankest kind of un-Americans—who are anxious to see the United States and Russia come to blows. I do not deny that in the past Russia has given the United States some provocation—just as the United States has given provocation to Russia. But anyone who has studied the relations of western Europe and Poland with Soviet Russia after World War I—anyone acquainted with the bungling policy of nonrecognition blindly followed by this country until Franklin Roosevelt ended it in 1933—surely can understand the background of Russian suspicions. However, there is no need here to unearth this past. The job for all of us today is to try to understand the basic historical, geographical, political, and economic facts. Then, I am sure, we would all readily understand the basic lack of conflict between the United States and the USSR—and then there would need be no question about our doing our part toward developing a co-operative and harmonious relationship with Russia. I am assuming, of course, that the Russians will come halfway. I think they will. From what I have learned through long and hard study of the Soviet Russian mind in action —from my own personal acquaintanceship with a wide range of Russian citizens from officials to factory workers— I firmly believe that the people of Russia have a great admiration and friendship for the people of the United States and that they want to live with us and prosper with us in peace.

Of course, the Russian system of government is not for us. It is probable that the Russian government will not, for a number of years, permit its citizens certain basic freedoms that we prize so dearly. But the Russians undoubtedly feel now that without Stalin and the Soviet system, Russia would have been destroyed in this war. I am also certain that the Russians, just like the rest of us, want to be sure that the peace is made secure. We must respect the Russian attitude—and they also must respect our own attitude with regard to preserving our own form of government. It is this mutual respect that means peace—that brings the certainty of peace. If we are to have a fuller life for all in the United States we must have this certainty of peace. We must not allow those who have personal grudges to settle to goad us into an unfriendly attitude. The world looks to its great powers for co-operation and for political, economic, and moral leadership, not for suspicion, hate, and war.

Finally, let us remember that we have nothing to fear from Communism in this country if our free-enterprise system lives up to its opportunities. Let us prosper with our own democratic system at home—and let us prosper with those abroad who, no matter what system they want or have, still want and strive to live in a nonaggressive peace with the rest of the world.

Civilization, emerging from this war, has won its right to one more chance for permanent peace. It may not have another.

II

Setting the Sights

FRANKLIN D. ROOSEVELT first set forth the nation's post-war goal of 60 million jobs in his challenging speech at Soldiers Field in Chicago on the night of October 28, 1944. The lessons learned from twelve years of close association with this great practical humanitarian should have cautioned me against questioning his goals. But just the same, my first feeling was that he had set his sights somewhat high. And that night I telegraphed him as follows:

YOUR GOAL OF SIXTY MILLION JOBS IS PERHAPS HIGH BUT
I GLORY IN YOUR DARING. AND, AS YOU SAY, AMERICA CAN
DO THE SEEMINGLY IMPOSSIBLE. WE ARE PREDICTING YOU
WILL CARRY THIRTY-SIX STATES AND HAVE A THREE-MIL-
LION POPULAR MAJORITY.

All that late summer and early fall, I had been campaigning day and night through the Middle West for the
Roosevelt-Truman ticket. In big city and country town—
and particularly in industrial centers—I had found widespread anxiety over the future of employment. But after
the Soldiers Field address, as I continued my campaigning
on into the East, I noted the immediate encouragement
given by Franklin Roosevelt's words. He had given his
pledge that government would not shirk its responsibility
to all of the people. And that pledge, alone, was sufficient
to give people a new faith in their future. The man who
made that pledge is dead. But we must justify his faith. We
must do this not for the sake of redeeming the pledge of
Franklin Roosevelt. We must do this to justify our faith
in ourselves and our country.

In the months since that Election Day, I have spent
more than half my time studying the mechanics of full
postwar employment. I have drawn upon the vast and
splendid statistical storehouse of the Federal agencies, and
upon the excellent resources of such nongovernmental
agencies as the National Planning Association and the
Committee for Economic Development—both devoted to
planning for freedom; and I have discussed all phases of
the problem with those in and out of government who

WE HAVE BECOME A NATION
OF 60 MILLION JOBS

Million jobs

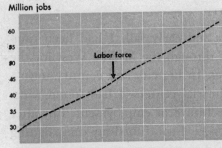

The number of people available for work has been steadily increasing. The U. S. Census estimates there will be over 62 millions by 1950.

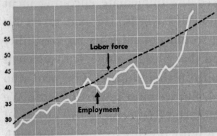

Actual employment follows closely the trend of the labor force, but in the 1930's it fell far short. In war years such as 1918 and 1944 many people normally outside the labor force are drawn into war jobs.

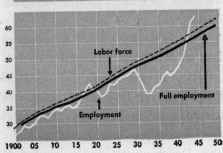

For full employment in 1950 we shall need jobs for 60 million people.

10

WE HAVE BECOME A
200 BILLION DOLLAR NATION

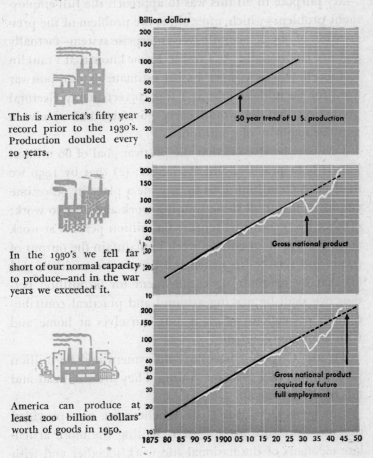

Billion dollars

This is America's fifty year record prior to the 1930's. Production doubled every 20 years.

50 year trend of U S. production

In the 1930's we fell far short of our normal capacity to produce—and in the war years we exceeded it.

Gross national product

America can produce at least 200 billion dollars' worth of goods in 1950.

Gross national product required for future full employment

1875 80 85 90 95 1900 05 10 15 20 25 30 35 40 45 50

11

have concerned themselves with finding an equitable an-swer—including representatives of business, agriculture, and labor.

My purpose in all this was to approach the full-employment problem—which, after all, is the problem of the preservation of our democratic free-enterprise system—factually and not emotionally. As a result, I now know that Franklin Roosevelt was as correct in his estimate of our postwar need for 60 million jobs as I was correct in my electoral prediction that he would carry 36 states and receive a popular majority of 3 million.

I do now believe (1) that the postwar goal of 60 million jobs is both practical and attainable; (2) that by 1950 we shall need 60 million jobs to provide a place in peacetime employment for all those wanting work and able to work; (3) that by 1950 it will require 60 million persons at work at an average of 40 hours a week to maintain the output of goods and services to which the people are entitled; and (4) that by maintaining employment for 60 million persons, we shall be making a sound and practical contribution to permanent peace, among ourselves at home and with all nations abroad.

To me, then, full postwar employment and 60 million jobs are one and the same thing. They are the head and tail of the same coin.

Can we achieve this goal? I believe we can—provided that the "pressure groups" representing the more articulate elements of the national life work together and with government for the common good of all of the people; and *provided that we act in time.*

But to win the peace, our sights must be set as high as they have been to win the war. We all recall that there were those who scoffed when Franklin Roosevelt, immediately following Pearl Harbor, established the goal of 50 thousand planes a year. We know now how right he was. It would be just as dangerous now to set our sights lower than 60 million postwar jobs as it would have been then to set our sights lower than 50 thousand planes a year. To talk of 50 million jobs is to talk of perpetuating mass unemployment and eventual chaos.

I think of this peace of abundance we must build as the People's Peace—and its foundation has already been laid for us. Franklin Roosevelt laid the foundation with the solid blocks of his Bill of Economic Rights. As set forth in his Address on the State of the Nation in January, 1944, these rights are:

The right to a useful and remunerative job in the industries or shops or farms or mines of the nation;

The right to earn enough to provide adequate food and clothing and recreation;

The right of every farmer to raise and sell his products at a return which will give him and his family a decent living;

The right of every businessman, large and small, to trade in an atmosphere of freedom from unfair competition and domination by monopolies at home or abroad;

The right of every family to a decent home;

13

The right to adequate medical care and the opportunity to achieve and enjoy good health;

The right to adequate protection from the economic fears of old age, sickness, accident, and unemployment;

The right to a good education.

These rights, however, are more than just the essentials of the People's Peace. They show us the scope of our job. They present to our democratic free-enterprise system the challenge of making the much-vaunted American standard of living a reality for *all* of our people. And only by meeting this challenge equitably and immediately and boldly—only by thinking positively now about mass consumption instead of negatively fearing mass unemployment—can our free way of life survive.

As a nation we have built to the limit of our geographical frontiers. Certainly, we must concern ourselves more and more, if we are to be a prosperous people, with building a realistic basis of sharing in the development of the frontiers abroad—in making foreign trade something more than our own one-way street. But most important of all, we must think about ourselves. We must do something about bringing the bottom half of our population within the boundaries of our economic frontiers at home. Moreover, by the very process of making it possible for all of our people to enjoy decent housing, better health, and a good education—by making it possible for all of our people to have the things that represent the fruit of their labor

—we will be providing more of the job opportunities for our full postwar employment.

But this achievement of the People's Peace—through increasing the purchasing power of the masses of the people —is the long-term problem. V-E Day forced upon us the *immediate* problem of carrying on reconversion with a minimum of dislocation and disruption even as we carried our fight through to final victory against Japan.

To win the war, government has had to assume virtually an absolute domination of the economy. To win the peace, we must get rid of this government domination of the economic structure as rapidly as possible—but with equal rapidity we also must determine the areas of responsibility in providing for full employment in the transition from war to peace. What are the exact responsibilities of government—Federal, state, and local? What are the responsibilities of the business community, of agriculture and labor? What is the responsibility of the local community?

It was in the interest of helping to clarify these responsibilities that Franklin Roosevelt supported the proposal for a unified national budget as a practical means of charting our total production for peace. To him, the present limited Federal budget belonged to the horse-and-buggy era. He realized that the total number of job opportunities in any one year must depend upon the total amount spent for goods and services by all of the consumers, by industry and business, and by government (Federal, state, and local). And he believed that only by giving periodic comprehensive estimates of the overall purchasing power of the entire nation could we know exactly where we stood, all of us, at any one time—just exactly what was ahead of us, and what measures by private enterprise and government might be required to maintain full employment.

Upon Franklin Roosevelt's death, Harry Truman inherited the massive burden of leading us in the search for the just and sound answers to these questions. He deserves to have the support of all fair-minded people, in and out of government. There will be differences, of course, over exact methods—for we are a democratic people. But we cannot afford differences over the size and immediacy of the job to be done.

This book explains my own ideas as to the necessary responsibilities for attaining and maintaining full employment—and as to the nature of the power which the people should assign to government and which, as businessmen and consumers, the people should keep for themselves. I have not attempted to give the exact specifications of just what we should do and how we should do it. In our democratic life, that is the function of the Congress. Rather I have tried to give some sense of direction to what I consider to be our needs as a people—the needs of all of our people. And I have tried to drive home the fact that the American people will never be satisfied if we produce less and consume less than our possibilities. From now on, the people will ask: Are we living up to our possibilities? Are we using all our resources, manpower, and knowledge? Are we working as hard to increase the standard of living of our own people as we did to destroy the cruel might of the master racist aggressors?

I believe that it will take approximately 60 million jobs by around 1950 to double the standard of living of those whose standard of living has been lowest; and that as a result of this doubling process, the rest of us will have our own incomes made more certain, and we all will have the satisfaction of living in a broadly based democracy for the first time.

There is danger involved, to be sure. But it is not the danger of losing our freedom through planning for freedom, as some would have us believe. It is not the danger that democratic planning will lead us unwittingly to "the servile state," to "the compulsory state," or to "the road to serfdom." This is the deliberate claptrap of confusionists.

Instead, the danger is that we shall not appreciate the all-important fact that it will be fully as difficult, fully as demanding of our patriotism, to win the peace as it was to win the war. It may be even more difficult.

That is the danger I see ahead. That is the danger we can avert only by realizing the price we shall have to pay if we fail.

III

The High Cost of Failure

M EN WITH broken spirits, women waiting at home in endless anguish, children neglected and undernourished—these are the true costs of unemployment.

All too many millions of American families have paid these terrible costs.

Savings vanish; and men walk the silent streets from shop to shop, from one closed factory gate to another, and succeed only in wearing out shoe leather. Pantry shelves are bare and chimneys smokeless; and wives and children join the search for work, any kind of work to earn the necessary penny, but only in vain. Both bodies and souls are weakened; and crime and disease increase as the bread lines lengthen. No one will ever be able to plumb the depths of tragedy that result when futility and frustration replace human dignity in a man's soul.

The most prized asset that any of us can have is the sense of belonging: the feeling that we are a part of something, that we are appreciated, that our efforts do count, that we can look ahead with mutual hope and confidence.

The impact of war on our security gave this sense of belonging to most of us. It gave us the feeling that we were bound together in a common endeavor for survival. The great problem of peace is to make it seem as important and as urgent as war.

We must feel as close to each other in winning the peace

18

THE HIGH COST OF UNEMPLOYMENT

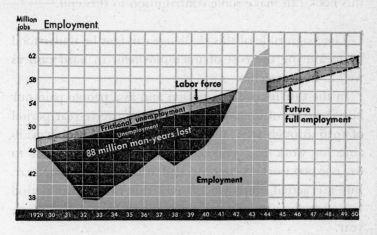

Million jobs Employment

Labor force

Frictional unemployment

Unemployment

88 million man-years lost

Employment

Future full employment

1929 30 31 32 33 34 35 36 37 38 39 40 41 42 43 44 45 46 47 48 49 50

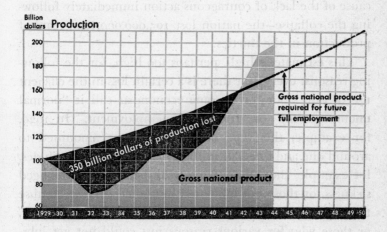

Billion dollars Production

350 billion dollars of production lost

Gross national product

Gross national product required for future full employment

1929 30 31 32 33 34 35 36 37 38 39 40 41 42 43 44 45 46 47 48 49 50

as we did in winning the war. We must make peace as challenging—and as exciting—as war. It is my hope that this book can make some contribution to this end.

The magnitude of this challenge can best be understood by measuring the cost of unemployment in hard cash as well as in heartaches.

In the thirties, we as a nation and as a people paid our heaviest costs of unemployment. In the twelve-year period of 1930 through 1941, the average number of people available for work was 52,000,000, or a total equivalent to 624,000,000 workers concentrated at their jobs in one year. But the actual employment over this twelve-year period was equivalent to only 519,000,000 people at work for one year.

Thus, because of the planlessness of the twenties—because of the lack of courageous action immediately following the collapse—the nation lost 105,000,000 man-years of production in the thirties.

This estimate is high, perhaps too high, for the following reasons: every year there is a certain loss in the efficient use of our labor force; some economists call it "normal unemployment" or "frictional unemployment." In 1929, for example, this type of unemployment amounted to around one and one-half million man-years. This includes, for example, those away from work because of prolonged sickness, or those not tabulated in annual surveys because they were in the midst of a shift from one job to another, or those who for various reasons just could not get jobs. Even at the peak of our war production, some 800,000 persons were included in this category of unemployment.

For the twelve years of unemployment, then, the sub-traction of this normal loss of about a million and a half annually from the labor force would leave a depression cost of 88,000,000 man-years.

To the national product, on the basis of present prices, these 88,000,000 lost man-years meant a loss of around 350 billion dollars.

The mind of man reels under the impact of such a sum; we find it difficult to realize just how much it really is, in terms of things we understand.

It is enough to pay in full for 70,000,000 homes at $5000 each—more than three times as many as would be necessary to eliminate all the slums in the United States, both urban and rural.

It is enough to more than double the capital stock of all the private corporations in the United States.

It is enough to build 350 river-valley authorities of the size of TVA.

And, as a final example, it is more than the Federal debt will be on V-J Day.

How did our system of free enterprise survive such a breakdown in production? Frankly, I am one of those who believe that we survived only because the bold, courageous action of the Roosevelt New Deal restored the people's confidence in themselves and their faith in their free in-stitutions. Bolstered by this rebirth of faith, the nation surged onward toward a broader base for our economic life. Time and again, the people gave overwhelming approval of the progressive leadership in Washington—and gave their mandate for more progress. We made greater social-economic gains in the years 1933 through 1941 than in any previous administration in our history. But all the while, the forces of aggression throughout the world also surged onward toward inevitable global war. Then, even before the end of the thirties, our progress was seriously interrupted. We must now pick up where we left off then, consolidate the gains, and develop a practical means of preventing mass unemployment.

In this process, we must shun the alarmist. But we need to keep ourselves informed of the dangers ahead, and be constantly concerned about them. As early as 1943, the Department of Commerce pointed out to us that, in 1946, we could produce the same amount of goods that we produced in 1940 and still have 19 million workers unemployed. All too often we ignore such statistical guideposts. Later on we look around and say, "We were warned. Why didn't we act before it was too late?"

Such guideposts point to this one inescapable fact: if we do not prepare our plans now, with courage and wisdom, we shall eventually experience a loss not of 88,000,000 man-years of labor but of 200,000,000 man-years of labor— a loss not of 350 billion dollars in national production, but a loss of more than 500 billion dollars.

It is anyone's guess as to what would happen to our free institutions once they were subjected to such joblessness and misery and waste.

Such, then, is the challenge the people must accept in the common endeavor to win the peace.

PART TWO

The Sixty Million Jobs

I

The Component Parts

SOME CRITICS of the goal of 60 million jobs are honest enough but are just naturally timid. Others pay sly lip service to full employment—but actually, they would tolerate several million permanently unemployed in the unsound belief that the competition of the unemployed will keep wages down and profits up.

Such people, in effect, look at unemployment as something like the old-fashioned game of "musical chairs"—with the rules of the business game set so that a certain number of people automatically would always be left out in the scramble for jobs. To them, the only question is, how many are to be left over?—not how can we avoid the ruination that unemployment brings to individuals and to the whole of our society.

The goal of 60 million jobs is based on the opposite premise—one which doesn't accept the idea that a large body of the citizenry should be denied jobs. This premise asserts that all those who want to work and seek work have a right to work. It says that, for the time being, 60 million jobs will provide work for all the people in the labor force in the country—except for those who at any one time are in transition from one job to another, or are in the "fric-

25

tional unemployed" for other reasons. It includes those who had jobs before the war; those who were unemployed then but have since found jobs and want to keep them; those who have been added to the labor force because of normal population growth; and those employed in the armed services. Sixty million jobs, of course, is not a final figure. It will be about right for 1949 through 1951 or 1952, but by 1955 it probably will be too small.

Actually, there will be more than 60 million in the labor force by 1950, for it is estimated that as many as 2 million of those who have been drawn into war work out of homes and schools may decide to continue as workers But if we take into account about 1½ million who are normally not working even in prosperity years—again the so-called "frictional unemployed"—we come back to the 60 million persons in the 1950 labor force for whom we need 60 million job opportunities. An average of 60 million persons at work at all sorts of jobs, including military service, would be no larger for 1950, when our population of 14 years of age and over will be 110 millions, than the average of 49 million persons at work was in 1929, when our population of 14 years of age and over was only 90 millions— just under 55 per cent at work in both cases.

THE MORE STABLE PARTS

Some well-meaning people talk as if they thought all the 60 million job opportunities would have to be found in manufacturing alone, or in agriculture and trade and construction. Their apprehension will disappear, I am sure, if we take a close look at the 60 million to see in what industries they are all likely to be working for pay or profit; and in what industries jobs would be most insecure if we should return to "normalcy."

On the basis of past experiences and fairly obvious trends in our requirements, I would expect that about 23 million of the 60 million job opportunities would lie in agriculture; in domestic service; and in the category of self-employed business and professional men, and salaried managers and officials; and in government (Federal, state, and local), and the armed services. (See Chart, pp. 42-43.)

These 23 million job opportunities would be divided roughly as follows:

Government and the armed forces would supply about	7,000,000 jobs
Agriculture would supply about	8,000,000 jobs
Domestic service would supply about	2,000,000 jobs
Self-employed (business and professional men) managers and officials would supply about	6,000,000 jobs
Total	23,000,000 jobs

In 1940, slightly more than 4 million workers were employed by Federal, state, and local governments. During the war, civilian employment in all three branches has increased to almost 6 million. There will be and should be retrenchments in this field of employment. I would say that from 4½ to 5 million would seem to be a reasonable estimate for the number of postwar jobs in government. As for the size of the armed services after total victory, no final estimate is yet available. But there seems to be some agreement that the permanent peacetime service strength will be, of necessity, in the neighborhood of 2½ million men. The total of 7 million, then, would be a reasonable figure for government and the armed services combined.

The estimate of 8 million postwar jobs in agriculture is about 2 million below the prewar figure, and approximately the same as the present number working on farms. Agricultural employment may rise a little from wartime levels as farm boys return from the service. But it is not likely, barring mass unemployment, to reach the prewar level. Great numbers of farm boys and girls will continue to seek careers in the cities.

Two million servants in the homes after the war is a little higher than the number employed in domestic service during the war years—but not as high as the number who crowded into this field during the depression, when better-paying jobs elsewhere were not available.

The estimate of 6 million in self-employment (which includes business proprietors and independent professional men), and in the managerial group, completes the breakdown of the 23 million jobs listed in the table set forth above—leaving 37 million jobs for which we must account. But this 6 million is much more significant to the sum total of 60 million jobs than is indicated in any routine categorical breakdown. For about one half of the

6 million comprise the employer group—those who do the hiring and firing—those who must either employ directly or determine the business policies effecting the employment of the remaining 37 million persons.

THE LESS STABLE PARTS

And for these 37 million persons—their opportunities for jobs must lie in manufacturing and mining, construction, transportation and other utilities, trade of all kinds, and finance, entertainment, and the service industries (hotels, restaurants, garages, service stations, laundries, barber shops and beauty parlors, cleaning and dyeing establishments, et cetera). These industries, particularly manufacturing, mining, and construction, are the volatile fields of employment. The rates of employment in these fields are the highly nervous indices to business confidence. If manufacturing and mining and construction fall sharply, there is an instantaneous response in the remaining fields of enterprise. And although I believe that the final distribution of full employment will not vary much from the breakdowns herein set forth, I want to emphasize that new inventions and techniques may change the competitive situation in those fields in many ways.

To provide and maintain employment for these 37 million persons, we must find markets for the products of 18 million people at work in manufacturing, mining, and construction. If there is a market for the products they make—markets either at home or abroad—then employment in these fields would average about as follows:

Manufacturing and mining	15	million
Construction	3½	million
Utilities and transportation	3½	million
Trade	9	million
Finance, services, and miscellaneous	6	million
Total	37	million

It is in manufacturing, construction, and mining where the ups-and-downs have been most violent. In manufacturing we have expanded most during the war. Here unemployment hits soonest and hardest. Back in the depression, in 1932, there were only about 6 million workers in the factories. In both 1929 and 1940 there were more than 10 million, and in 1943 at the war peak, the figure was almost 17 million. After the war it seems reasonable to expect at least 14 million jobs in manufacturing.

Mining will provide about 1 million postwar jobs. This is about the same as the 1929 figure and a little higher than the 1940 figure. Thus we must have a total of 15 million in manufacturing and mining. Fewer than 14 million in these two fields means the beginning of mass unemployment. Fifteen million or more mean prosperity.

On a percentage basis, construction will have the greatest expansion in postwar employment. Ever since Pearl Harbor, private construction activity has been stringently limited, and since the completion of the service camps and bases, employment in the whole field has dropped to about a half million—even less than it was at the bottom of the Great Depression. I believe that enough need for construction of all kinds, public and private, exists in this country to provide jobs for from 3 to 3½ million workers annually in the years immediately after the war. Several persons who closely follow construction needs tell me I may be low in this estimate. If I am, so much the better for all of us.

Transportation and public utilities can be expected to provide from 3½ to 4 million postwar jobs. This is slightly higher than the number in 1940 and very little different from the 1929 figure. Railroad workers' jobs depend directly on activity in manufacturing, mining, and construction.

The number of jobs in trade is directly dependent upon the prosperity of the rest of the workers. In 1929 there were about 6 million people working in trade (that is, clerks, bookkeepers, salesmen, and similar employees in wholesale and retail establishments, importing and exporting firms, et cetera). Even in war years, with gas stations, auto salesrooms, etc., mostly closed down, the figure has been about 7 million. With full employment after the war, and with the restoration of the shorter prewar work week, it is reasonable to expect about 9 million such jobs in trade.

The remaining 6 million jobs will be scattered in the fields of finance, the services, industries, amusements, and miscellaneous activities. In 1929 about 4 million people were employed in these categories. At the height of war production this figure was less than 4 million, but the war made it impossible for many people who wanted to hire such workers to find them. With full employment and shorter working hours after the war, I would anticipate a demand for 5 and probably 6 million people in this field.

These estimates of the breakdown of full employment, of course, will be challenged by some. Instead of the 37 million jobs needed, they will point out that in 1940, these fields of employment—from manufacturing to the service industries—provided employment for only 25 million persons and that we cannot expect much more than that in the postwar years.

But to me the real point is this: I am sure that no sensible man in business, just as no sensible man in government, wants to accept 1940 as a normal year. I have never accepted the unemployment of 1939 or 1940 as something we must live with in this land of limitless opportunities. Nor will I accept it now.

Those who talk of 50 million jobs as full employment are really talking for a national income of at least 35 billion dollars less than we can earn provided only that we have the courage to produce and consume the goods the people really want and need. I refuse to accept this loss of 35 billion dollars in national income as inevitable. It is only by producing this additional 35 billion dollars a year that we can pay for this war without imposing too costly a burden upon our economy. Fifty million jobs are just not enough when the labor force is more than 60 millions. It is insanity to think that we can pay for this war by throwing people out of work.

In moving from war to peace, we must be prepared for rapid changes. There will be dislocations in many areas and industries. The peace fronts will demand sudden changes just as did the war fronts. Not only the labor force but also the men in management must be ready for rapid shifts—both from one industry to another and from one geographical region to another.

There are two industries which are strategic in the sense that their attainment of full employment in civilian production will lead the way to full employment in other fields—and also in the sense that they are areas in which government policies and operations will be basic to the achievement of full employment.

One is manufacturing, where government can either accelerate or choke off the reconversion process—where it can either help to keep 14 million people employed or can precipitate a decline which will be extremely difficult to check. The other is construction, where the government can act, and has traditionally acted, directly, to create employment in the construction of needed public works.

To put full employment on a continuing basis means that the people, through the Congress, must equip government with authority to act in immediate co-operation with private enterprise once incipient unemployment points to the danger of mass unemployment. There are honest differences of opinion, of course, as to just when we reach the danger point of unemployment in our economy. In our previous years of short-lived full employment, as already noted, we had from 1½ to 2 million unemployed (due to technological progress, to seasonal unemployment

33

in construction or other trades, and to normal changes from one job to another). I believe that we should not tolerate any wider margin even with a labor force of 62 million—the total our population statistics now indicate for 1950. This suggests that if the total of civilian and military jobs falls below 59 million, then there is real cause for concern—and if the total falls below 58 million we must beware of serious trouble.

WHO WILL HAVE THE JOBS

But what about the people themselves—those who will fill these 60 million jobs? Who are they? What do we know about them?

The bulk of the 60 million will be workers between the ages of 20 and 65; nearly 55 million will be included in this age group. In addition, about 3 million will be boys and girls under 20, including some full-time workers who have finished school, and some students earning their way with part-time jobs. Roughly 2 million will be men and women over 65. These estimates for workers over 65 and under 20 are based on the assumption that there will be a sharp decrease in the proportions of people working at such ages, in line with the trends toward longer schooling and earlier retirement.

Of the 60 million about 48 million will be native whites, about 6 million will be foreign-born whites, and about 6 million will be Negroes. There will be approximately 42 million men and 18 million women. Before the war, 11 million women were at work in income-earning jobs. Many of the 3 million women, young and old, who have been drawn into war work will return to their homes and schools. But at least a million and perhaps a million and one half will want to continue in paying jobs.

The women working after the war will be mainly in the age group of 20 to 44 years. About 12 million out of the 18 million working women will be in this age class. They will be mostly single women or married women without children. After the war, as before, it is expected that very few mothers of young children will be at work outside of the home.

About 14 of the 60 million will be organized, and about 46 million unorganized—and union strength will continue to vary industry by industry. Less than 15 per cent of clerical workers are organized, and only 20 per cent of the service workers. In manufacturing, the proportion organized is 60 per cent; in construction and transportation, over 80 per cent; in coal mining, shipping, and railroad transportation, it is about 95 per cent. Full employment, however, may speed up somewhat the organization of workers in unorganized fields, just as wartime activity speeded up their organization in manufacturing.

These are some of the realities and characteristics of the people who will fill the 60 million jobs in 1950 if the necessary job opportunities are provided. There is nothing mythical about them, either in toto or in breakdown. They are based on the Census.

II

The Interdependence of the Parts

I HAVE SAID that the goal of 60 million jobs is attainable
—provided that the "pressure groups" co-operate for
the common good. This may be a big "if." True enough, it
is. But it is also a realistic and not a wishful "if."

There can be no lasting full employment in any one
group or area of our national life unless there is lasting
full employment in all. Our common survival as a free
and democratic people rests upon the realization of our
economic interdependence. Economic exploitation by one
group or a coalition of groups, supported by political exploitation, can succeed for a time without despoiling our
free economic system. But there is always an end—a sad
end even for most of the exploiters. Our history is filled
with "Black Fridays"—and they have had a relentless way
of getting bigger and sadder. It is an intolerably dangerous
process. But we are continually being pushed along this
dangerous path by those who scoff at the goals we ought to
establish for our own security.

To get the meaning of the economic interdependence of
the groups in our national life—to see what the goal of 60
million jobs means to each group and what the groups
mean to each other—let us have a brief look at some of
these groups.

WHAT FULL EMPLOYMENT MEANS
TO THE BUSINESSMAN

First, the businessman. There are 3 million of them who must give jobs to 37 million other people and whose policies and attitudes affect the employment of all.

He is the proprietor of the corner drugstore and the Chairman of the United States Steel Corporation. He manufactures and sells the whole multitude of the tools of production—such as blast furnaces and concrete mixers, rolling mills and brick kilns, tractors and threshing machines, wheat drills and corn cultivators, hoes and axes, and the forges and machine tools of an automobile assembly line. He builds your house and provides you with fuel, power, communication, and transportation. He hires labor; and he buys the farmer's products and processes them into food and clothing. And he puts labor to work to provide you with all the rest of the necessities and comforts of your daily life—radios and refrigerators, a good stove in the kitchen and a good heating plant in the basement, and all of the other conveniences of good living.

The businessman must be both visionary and practical. From his vision must come new and better products—and constant improvements in the American know-how. To translate his dreams into profits, he invests his money and stakes his business reputation—and runs all the risks of competition.

But what would the businessman do without the rest of us? For even though some of us may also be businessmen, all of us are customers—with varying degrees of purchasing power.

Whether big or small—whether he tends his butcher shop in his shirt sleeves or rules an industrial empire from his paneled office high in a New York skyscraper—the businessman needs all of us. He needs good customers, steady customers, and more of them. He needs an ever-expanding market.

The businessman, of course, will look abroad to expand his market. He should. But he should also remember the "foreign markets" within our own country. There are still plenty of undeveloped frontiers at home. Higher standards of living in foreign countries would mean new markets; but so would higher standards of living, say, in Mississippi or North Dakota—or in the slums of New York and Chicago.

We like to boast about the American standard of living. It is pictured for us in thousands of advertisements—the trim house with sunny rooms and tiled bath, children romping on the shady and well-kept lawn, and an automobile parked at the curb. The businessman fondly looks on America as a ready market for radios, wrist watches, and inner-spring mattresses—and choice cuts of meat and fancy groceries. Millions do enjoy such a standard.

But in 1940 more than one third of the nation's 37 million families had incomes of less than $1000 per year. As customers they were none too good even for such basic necessities as food. More than 10 million families had annual incomes between $1000 and $2000. They were fair customers for the basic necessities and even for mechanical

UPS AND DOWNS OF EMPLOYMENT
AFFECT US ALL

Level of employment determines . . .

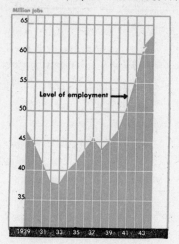

Workers' income . . .

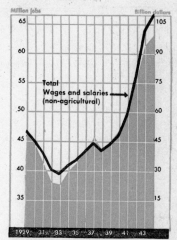

. . . Farmers' income . . .

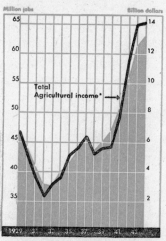

. . . and Business income

* Net income of farm operators and wages and salaries of farm workers.

** Corporate net income after taxes, net income of other business, and self-employed.

refrigerators and $20 suits. It is true that they took a tremendous part of our production, but none of them were as good customers as they should have been. In fact, at least three quarters of America's families have yet to play their full part as customers.

They can never play their full part as long as periodic mass unemployment creates violent fluctuations in their ability to buy the products of business. To be good customers they must be steady customers—and to be steady customers they must have steady jobs. It is a seamless web of cause and effect—an economic one world.

Throughout the war we have seen what mass consumption really means. We have produced more goods than we even hoped we could produce—and yet there have been constant and severe shortages. Why? Not only because of the tremendous food supplies sent overseas to our Armed Forces and those of our allies. Not only because we have helped to feed liberated peoples. But also and very largely because millions of people at home have had the money to buy more food, and better food, than they were ever able to afford before.

The cash registers in the grocery stores and meat markets in the poorer neighborhoods have rung up this profitable fact every day.

There are two ways of making money in business. The first way is to make a small number of sales at high prices with high profit margins. Many men have been successful in this kind of business. But sooner or later one of two things happens: either they are driven out by competition, or they join in monopolistic agreements to eliminate competition.

The other way of making money in business is the way that has come to be the backbone of America's economic strength. It is the way of greater production at lower prices, more efficiency, and higher wages for a huge mass market. To me, this is American business in action. No wage is too high if the worker earns it. Five cents an hour is too high if the worker doesn't earn it.

In 1926, for example, the average price of a mechanical refrigerator was $400—and in that year, some 200,000 units were sold. But ten years later, the industry was making a much better product selling at an average of only $160— and in that year it sold two million refrigerators.

And what about radios? Again in 1926, the industry sold 1,750,000 sets at an average price of $114 a set. Ten years later the industry sold 8,500,000 sets at an average price of $54.50 per set. And by 1941, the total units sold reached 13,000,000 at an average price of $35. This figure, of course, includes the bedside models as well as the costly cabinet sets; but also included are all of the accumulated technical improvements of an electronics age.

In both the radio and refrigerator industries—in automobiles and washing machines, and in a variety of other lines—the tabulation of statistics spells out the same story of increased profits through increased sales at lower prices.

As a result of the wartime curtailments, there is a tremendous accumulated consumer demand, including at the end of 1944: 11 million passenger automobiles—41 million radios—1 million sewing machines—82 million clocks and watches—10 million refrigerators—6 million washing machines—17 million electric irons—and 8 million toasters.

These accumulations, however, represent only the demand of those families which were already established within our economic frontiers—from families with incomes over $1500 a year. Thus, any real expansion of markets must come from the increased purchasing power of those families which, before the war, were in the lowest income groups.

Before the war one third of all families had incomes of less than $1000, averaging about $500; another 40 per cent had incomes between $1000 and $2000, averaging $1400; another 17 per cent had incomes between $2000 and $3000; and the final 10 per cent had incomes of over $3000.

During the war the whole scale of distribution of family income has moved upward, and if this gain can be maintained after the war, we shall have only half the percentage of families with incomes under $1000 we had before the war, and a great increase in the proportion with incomes between $2000 and $4000.

This is an example of the increased purchasing power the businessman needs for expansion of his markets. This is the upward trend we must maintain with continued full employment in the peace to come—this is what makes more and better customers. And with this increased national income that results from continued full employment at good wages, the businessman enters upon a prosperous cycle of opportunities.

He has the opportunity for both a steadier volume of sales and a more stable profit. In 1929, the total net profits after taxes of all corporations were 7 billion dollars—while three years later these same corporations showed a total net loss of half a billion dollars. Facing both the risk of competition and the risk of mass unemployment, the businessman, in the past, has feasted against the day of famine. And we all know, from past experiences, whither that practice leads us.

This assurance of more stable profits, in turn, means more opportunities for new investments, for the development of new products and new industries. With full employment and 200 billion dollars in national production there would be opportunities for twice the annual investment or use of savings that we had in 1929.

FROM 47 MILLION JOBS IN 1940 . . .

Distribution of U. S. workers

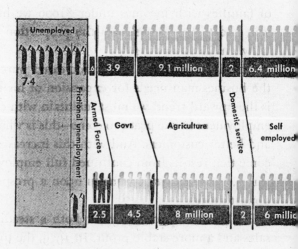

Full employment also means more opportunity for the small businessman. In years of good business, the small businessman can stand up to the big one; but when hard times come, the big fellow has all the advantages. The record of past depressions shows that all too often the little fellow was forced into bankruptcy through no fault of his own.

Before the war, there were some 3 million little businesses in this country—employing three men or less, and engaged in retail trade, small-job contracting, laundering, auto-servicing, and the like. Such businesses as these are the very heart of our free-enterprise system. During the war, half a million of these disappeared due to wartime

. . . TO 60 MILLION JOBS IN 1950

(see page 27)

by major occupation groups

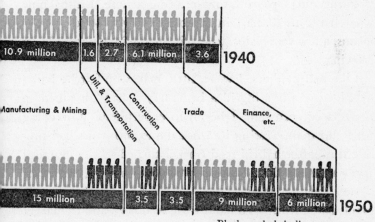

10.9 million   1.6   2.7   6.1 million   3.6   **1940**

Manufacturing & Mining   Util. & Transportation   Construction   Trade   Finance, etc.

15 million   3.5   3.5   9 million   6 million   **1950**

Black symbols indicate
proposed increases in employment

conditions. But if we are to maintain our free-enterprise system, it is essential not only that the half million should be re-established—but also that we have several hundred thousand new enterprises of this size. Fortunately, the fact is that full employment conditions by 1950 will provide opportunities for around a million more people in self-employment.

The small business and the family-sized farm have always been and must continue to be the seed bed of American democratic free enterprise. Full employment will give the little fellow the chance he needs; then it is up to him to make the best use of the flexibility, the initiative and the enterprise that come from youth.

I know a little something about the problem of beginning a business—both from the visionary standpoint of the idea and the practical standpoint of raising the capital, sweating out a payroll, and meeting a note. I also know what it means to start in a prosperous year—and what it means, a few years later, to survive hard times and keep on growing.

Like many others, I was a little man who felt he had a new idea—really a big idea in its way. I had "dreamed" a better seed corn—and I began to experiment, inbreeding corn and then crossing it. Once the experiments had produced a better hybrid seed corn, I turned to the practical application of the idea. With Simon Cassady, Jr., I designed the first modern seed-corn drying and processing plant in the world. To handle the seed corn and to market it, I organized a company and raised the capital myself.

That was in 1926. I was president and general manager until I came to Washington in 1933. The company now has plants in Iowa, Illinois, Indiana, and Ohio—and we sell four million dollars' worth of seed corn a year.

Moreover, I not only established a business but played a considerable part in starting a new industry. Our company now has three large competitors; in addition, several thousand farmers either produce small amounts of hybrid seed corn which they sell in their own localities, or else act as local distributors for one of the four companies.

This, I know, is a commonplace business experience. Every day, as Secretary of Commerce, I meet businessmen who could buy and sell our own company before breakfast. I met them, too, as Secretary of Agriculture and as Vice-President—only I probably meet more of them now. However, my own experience taught me what ticks inside the little man with the big idea—the little man who puts the big idea into practical use for a profit and thereby creates job opportunities for others.

For many years, I have written and spoken of the new opportunities for business—the new frontiers of economic development. Throughout these years, I have wondered why so many so-called practical business leaders still lived according to the economic textbooks of a bygone era. I have wondered why so many have staked their chance for survival on high prices, low wages, and a subnormal volume of business—on gorging in good times to live through the bad.

This is a negative and undemocratic business philosophy. It is the philosophy of those who believe that ours is a mature economy—who believe that the economic frontiers were closed with the closing of our geographic frontiers. It denies our economic interdependence and the opportunities inherent in the very thing that has made ours a great industrial nation—mass production for mass consumption. And this at a time when we have only begun to scratch the surface of our opportunities for mass consumption.

If this business view were to prevail, then business would be fighting only a rearguard action—it would be making a steady retreat and leaving the field to the forces of totalitarianism.

But I also know enough business leaders, big and small, who refuse to accept this philosophy of scarcity to give me hope and courage and strength in my job—both as a government official and as a private citizen. And all of us, no matter what our job is, or how big or important it is, need such strength of mutual belief and mutual stimulation of purpose. This book, then, is also an expression of my belief as a small businessman—and not just as a public servant—in the philosophy of abundance instead of scarcity.

WHAT FULL EMPLOYMENT MEANS
TO THE WORKER

Whether he runs a turret lathe on a production line or hustles cargo on the dock—whether he is a miner or a hired hand on the farm, a railroad man or a clerk in an insurance office, an oil-well driller or the driver of a laundry truck—whatever his job, the worker wants and must have the opportunity to a better job. He wants to realize the American dream of full opportunity for all.

He can have his chance only with full employment.

With full production for war, the worker gained the feeling of job security. He knew that if circumstances beyond his control deprived him of one job he could get another.

I have visited with workers in all parts of the country—in their shops and in their homes. I have seen their faces by the thousands in airplane plants and arsenals and shipyards. And upon those faces I have seen the looks not only of pride in their country but of the self-respect that comes from doing a job well and knowing the job still would be there the next day, the next month, the next year.

On these visits, I often thought of the heartless charge we heard so frequently only a few short years ago—"the unemployed don't want to work"—and I knew that the charge was only a cruel excuse for lack of action, a twisted defense of a failure or refusal to think in terms of full employment. Millions of workers who were jobless before regained their integrity and self-reliance in the war prosperity. But they cannot keep it unless peace is made as prosperous as war. And if they lose it, it will be the fault of all of us—not the fault of the workers.

Along with his wartime job security, the worker also has received both higher wages and higher take-home pay—although I believe that wages have increased considerably less than some persons would have us believe. In the munitions industries, wages have increased sharply and, with heavy overtime, the take-home pay often has risen spectacularly. But even in the munitions industries, many workers get much less than the highly publicized take-home totals of $100 and even $150 a week—while numerous other industries have continued to pay only prewar hourly rates plus the 15 per cent increase allowed by the "Little Steel Formula." Textile workers, tire-makers, foundry and forge workers, lumberjacks, and many other groups may actually have less money left at the end of the week than they did before the war because their living costs and taxes have risen faster than their wages.

Despite these qualifications, the fact still remains that wages and salaries in 1944 totaled almost 113 billion dollars as compared with about 49 billion dollars in 1940. More people at work, rises in hourly wage rates, the increase of overtime work and pay, the upgrading of workers —all have had their part in achieving this total increase. But I want particularly to stress the factor of full employment itself.

During the war millions of workers, for the first time, have had several years of continuous work at greater annual earnings. From this we get some idea, also for the first time, of what it would mean to the worker—and to the whole of the economy—if we could find the practical means of guaranteeing wages on an annual basis instead of forcing the worker to exist from a week-to-week or even a month-to-month basis. Several nationally known companies have been doing valuable spadework for some years in developing the annual wage policy on an annual basis. Today, it is heartening that the discussion of an annual wage, both by management and labor, now cuts across many lines of industry.

What the worker wants—and needs to have—is an opportunity to know that he can have a certain security in his job, and a certain purchasing power for himself and his family throughout the coming years. Continuation of full employment in peacetime—profiting from our wartime experiences—should make it possible to find more quickly the means of guaranteeing the annual wage in all industries in which it is feasible.

Collective bargaining, of course, also played a very important part in achieving these wage increases, though it is difficult to measure its effect in exact terms.

Whatever the relative weight of the various causes of the increases, we need to keep these high wage payments after the war. Only by doing this can we provide markets for the level of production we must have for full employment. We need to keep something very close to the present level of wage payments.

The war greatly expanded employment in the relatively high-paid metalworking industries. With reconversion, there will be a shift in employment back to textiles, clothing, the service industries, and numerous other lines which in the past usually have been low-wage industries. It will also mean an employment shift back to construction—which, though often high in wage rates, usually has been low in annual incomes. Therefore, if we are to maintain anything like the present levels of take-home pay, we must give realistic consideration to raising the levels of wages in these low-paid industries.

I have already referred to the Department of Commerce "guidepost" showing that, in 1946, we could produce as much as we did in 1940 and still have 19 million unemployed. This reflects directly our increased efficiency—our increased output per hour—a large part of the benefits of which must be passed on to the worker in the form of higher wages, or lower prices. But safety for all of us does not lie in trying to lower our wage and price structure. It lies, instead, in holding close to the present average level of prices *and* total wage payments.

Next to its high efficiency, the dominant characteristic of wartime labor has been its mobility. Labor, too, has been a mobile task force.

Millions of workers broke their home ties to take war jobs in distant cities. Whole trainloads of shipyard workers often sped across the continent to maintain production schedules.

This mobility on the home front was as essential as mobility on the war fronts. But it also has contributed considerably to the problems of reconversion. In California and Kansas, manufacturing employment has trebled during the war; in Washington, Nebraska, Texas and other states, it has doubled. To avoid having millions of workers stranded in areas of concentration in all parts of the country—such as those in and around Los Angeles and around San Francisco Bay—the same mobility must be exercised in the reconversion to peace.

The worker, I am sure, appreciates the fact that reconversion again requires widespread shifts in types of production and areas of production. He knows only too well that millions of workers again will be on the move during these shifts—moving to a different kind of job or to another area. He knows we could not possibly put to use in peacetime all of the increased capacities in, say, shipbuilding and airplane construction that were needed for war. He expects new dislocations and uprootings.

But the worker looks to government and industry to co-operate with labor to make the transition as short as possible—and to make certain (1) that the tools of production, old and new, which he used in war will, after the necessary shifts, be used to the fullest possible extent in peace; and (2) that new tools will be available, in old industries and new, to maintain continuous full employment.

In short, the worker wants and must have assurance that mobility in war will not lead to national immobility, industrial stagnation, and bread lines in peace.

In surveying what full employment has meant to the worker in wartime and can mean even more with full employment in peace, I want to emphasize these two basic gains: first, the advances made in elimination of discrimination in employment for reasons of race, religion, or sex; and second, the rise in labor-management co-operation.

Except for isolated instances, broad-minded and intelligent businessmen, themselves, long ago forced an end to discriminations against Catholics and Jews. But prejudice continued to exist quite generally against hiring women in manufacturing. And even in the war we still failed to make full use of the skills of the Negro.

In 1940 the labor force included 40 million men and 13 million women. During the next four years, while the number of men increased 5 million, or about 12 per cent, the number of women rose 4½ million, or about 25 per cent. Furthermore, the number of unemployed women (i.e., those in the labor force seeking but not finding jobs) dropped from 2 million in 1940 to less than half a million in 1944, so that the net gain in employment among women has been about 6 million. The proportion of women in nonagricultural jobs has increased from 28 per cent of the total in 1940 to 37 per cent of the total in 1944.

This increase does not merely reflect the wartime increase in the need for workers in general. It also shows that women proved in war production that they could do as well as men in many jobs and better than men in a few jobs. Now that they have wiped out the discrimination against them, it is estimated that almost half of the women who sought and found jobs during the war will keep them if given the opportunity to do so.

Negro employment likewise showed substantial increase during the war and considerable progress was made in upgrading of Negro labor to better paying jobs. In 1940, there were slightly fewer than 5 million Negroes employed in manufacturing; but by January, 1945, there were 8 million—an increase of 63 per cent. Continued full employment conditions would assure the opportunity to continue the progress we have made, not only in upgrading Negroes to better jobs but also in eliminating discriminatory wage differentials—provided we also make sure that the Fair Employment Practices Committee is placed on a permanent basis with power to bring its decisions to judicial review for enforcement.

In 1940 in one of our important rural industries, Negroes held 70 per cent of the jobs which paid less than 35 cents an hour, while white workers held more than 80 per cent of the jobs which paid more than 40 cents an hour. But this statement suggests that there is more racial wage discrimination than really exists. White people working under the same conditions and in the same jobs as the Negroes also got less than $15 a week.

There was a time when certain Southern leaders were proud of the South's low wage scale because they thought it served as an incentive to bring industry to the South. Today more and more of the thoughtful Southern leaders proclaim that the South is entitled to as high a wage scale as that in the North. More and more of them now advocate the education and training which will make Southern workers as efficient as those in the North. In doing this, these thoughtful Southerners are doing good service to the workers of all the country. For if both wages and efficiency can be raised to, and kept at, a level twice that of 1940, the South's great untapped market can become as important to us as the untapped markets overseas.

Labor-management co-operation is not, of course, a war-born idea. But it is only since March, 1942, when the War Production Board inaugurated its program of Labor-Management Production Committees, that figures have been available to indicate the extent of their accomplishments.

Between March, 1942, and December, 1944, a total of

nearly five thousand such committees, covering more than 7 million workers, had registered with WPB. Not all of them remained active and some of them existed only on paper. Yet according to WPB's tentative estimates, more than 200 million man-hours a year were gained as a result of the ideas submitted through or stimulated by these labor-management committees.

Improvements in design, stores control, maintenance, layout, lighting, quality improvement, interdepartmental relations, repair, and many other problems are listed in committee reports as benefits of this program.

Reading through some of these reports, I was particularly impressed by this comment from a manufacturing concern—a statement striking the theme of interdependence:

"We feel that the Labor Management Committee has been a real factor in improving our relations with the union—and thus, ultimately, the individual efficiency of the workers. Since this plan was put into operation, our records show that the production per worker has gone up over 25 per cent."

Another comment, also from management, strikes at the roots of community responsibility:

"The true value of these committees is to be sought as much as in the understanding that grows out of practicing co-operation as in their contribution to greater and better production."

Nothing could be of such benefit to the general welfare as the continued extension of this co-operation between management and labor in postwar production. Indeed,

54

here lies the very hope of gaining the national production so necessary to provide 60 million jobs. Management owes certain responsibilities to labor; and labor owes certain responsibilities to management. With mutual tolerance and understanding between these two groups in the difficult days ahead, we stand our best chance of getting good wages for labor, good prices for the farmer, stable profits for businessmen—and a higher standard of living for those who need it most.

WHAT FULL EMPLOYMENT MEANS
TO THE FARMER

I think I can qualify as an expert on this subject without too much challenge. The Wallaces always have tilled the land—in Scotland, in Ireland, in western Pennsylvania, and then out in Iowa. They always have been intimate with the problems of the farmer. And it seems they always were trying to do something about them.

As a boy I often listened as my father and grandfather talked with "Tama Jim" Wilson, who was Secretary of Agriculture from 1896 to 1912. It used to be said that my grandfather, who was known throughout Iowa as "Uncle Henry," could have had the Secretaryship when McKinley was elected in 1896—but he insisted that "Tama Jim" get the job. They often discussed such topics as freight-rate discrimination and the unfair practices forced on the farmer by the packing companies. Quite early in life, I came to know that the farmer had to sell his products in the world market at a world price, and buy his daily needs of life and his tools of production in a protected market. I remember when my father first told me about the "Iowa idea" of cutting the tariffs on the things farmers bought—and how he joined in the fight against the Payne-Aldrich tariff.

My father became Secretary of Agriculture in 1921. And when Franklin Roosevelt gave me the same job in 1933, I know how proud I was to see my father's portrait hanging on the wall in my office. I suppose I must have felt, then, a longing to see the portrait of "Uncle Henry" beside that of my father. I do know, though, that oftentimes in the almost eight years that I sat in that office, my thoughts could not help but go back to "Tama Jim" and "Uncle Henry" and my father. They taught me this one basic and kindly fact—the farmer, if he is worth the seed he sows, is a humanitarian.

Good farmers everywhere want to produce to the limit of good land management. They know they must protect their soil fertility and prevent soil erosion. They know that it is wise from time to time to give the land a rest. But they love the feel of the dirt—and they want to make things grow.

From my grandfather I learned at first hand what happened to the farmer after the Civil War—when farm prices swiftly and disastrously dropped 75 per cent. And I quickly came to understand the effects of the excessive ups-and-downs of industry and the stock market upon farm prices and land values. My first prediction was made in January, 1919, when I pointed to the danger signs ahead for agriculture—and set forth what I thought would happen if nothing were done. Again, in 1921, I urged the farmers in Iowa to cut down their corn acreage because it was apparent that the European demand for corn-and-hog products shortly would be cut in half, and because rising unemployment in this country would limit the domestic market.

In such emergency periods—or when a foreign market for a farm product has disappeared as a result of a high tariff policy—the farmer has as much reason as his city cousin in the manufacturing business to limit production. But he still doesn't like to do so.

From my own experiences with farm groups in all parts of the country, I am certain that our farmers, with comparatively few exceptions, would prefer to co-operate with industry for all-out production of industrial and farm products rather than to co-operate among themselves to try to work out a scarcity program of agriculture to match a scarcity program of industry. Surely, the farmer knows the meaning of group interdependence.

Back in NRA days, Hugh Johnson and I made a series of speeches on "The Two Legs of Prosperity—Factory Payrolls and Farm Income," showing the interdependence between farms and cities. We pointed out that when factory payrolls dropped from 11 billion dollars in 1929 to less than 5 billion dollars in 1932, farm incomes also dropped from 11 billion dollars to less than 5 billion dollars. To carry this parallel further—by 1937, when factory payrolls had risen to 10 billion dollars, farm income had risen to 9 billion dollars.

The Department of Agriculture has made a careful study of the relationship of full employment to increased consumption of farm products—showing that if there is full employment after the war, the average person will eat 96 pounds of pork products a year as compared with 67 pounds in the years of unemployment before the war. He will eat 25 pounds of chickens as compared with 18 pounds—and 75 pounds of oranges as compared with 49 pounds. He may not consume quite as much wheat and potatoes, but he will consume about 38 per cent more canned vegetables, 12 per cent more dairy products, and 17 per cent more eggs.

Contrariwise, 10 million postwar unemployed would cut the net income of the average farmer in half. The price of pork products, for example, would be cut in half —or else production would have to be reduced by about 40 per cent. Fifteen million postwar unemployed would mean a cut in net agricultural income to about one fourth of what it was in 1944. Farm labor, it's true, would be cheaper; for farm operators couldn't afford to pay decent wages, and the farm labor force would be increased by about a million farmers' sons and hired hands returning either from the Armed Services or from factory jobs that no longer existed. But the farmer would find no profit in this cheaper labor; for wages, and production and living costs in general, would not fall as rapidly as the price of the farmer's products.

All the foregoing does not mean, of course, that full employment would solve the farm problem in its entirety. There are also serious problems of getting the proper land use and of improving farm practices. For many years, one half of the nation's 6½ million farm families have been living on marginal and submarginal land and on farms too small to make a decent living. They have been producing only about 10 per cent of all the farm products sold in the market. Full employment in the cities will provide job opportunities in industry for some of these subsistence families, particularly in the South.

The small cotton farmer and the cotton sharecropper, for example, can expect trouble ahead even if there is no unemployment whatsoever. Full employment would increase the per capita consumption of cotton products by about 20 per cent; but that is far from being enough either to offset the loss in foreign markets due to the expanding production of cotton throughout the world or to offset the competition from rayon and other fibers at home.

For years to come the South will have to face the continuing necessity of re-examining its position, and using the co-ordinating power of the Federal government to adjust itself to changing world markets and to changed technologies. To a lesser extent, so will agriculture in the rest of the nation.

Even with full employment at present wage levels there would still be around 8 million city families getting less than $1000 a year. These families just would not be able to buy enough in the way of meat, eggs, and dairy products either to raise healthy children or to maintain their own vigor at a high pitch for high-class work.

For an all-too-brief period right before the war, the Surplus Marketing Administration's food-stamp plan remedied this situation somewhat by providing better food for those needing it, and markets for surplus farm products. But the stamp plan was confined to a limited number of areas and to a few commodities—and it covered, in most instances, only those families certified for relief or to certain other case-worked families. I recognize the administrative problems involved in extending this type of plan to all the lowest-income families over all the country on a permanent basis. Moreover, the administrative cost would be higher—inasmuch as the certifications under the stamp plan were all handled by relief and welfare agencies. But I still believe the goal is of such importance that we should give immediate postwar consideration to finding the most feasible system to increase food consumption by the lowest-income families—using again, as the stamp plan did, the regular retail channels of distribution.

The farmer, if he is wise, will give his fullest support to every practical endeavor of this type, including the expansion of school-lunch and free or low-cost milk programs—just as he will support labor's full employment at high wages. For the farmer prospers only as labor prospers. The lowest-income worker is just about as much a liability to the farmer as the unemployed worker.

Ordinarily, the agricultural population, with its higher birth rate, supplies workers to the cities. This is particularly true in prosperous years, when so many farm boys seek the better-paying jobs in Detroit, in Chicago or in other industrial centers. Consequently, when there is full employment in the cities, there will be from 1 to 2 million fewer people working on the farm than in bad years. But with 10 million unemployed in the cities—and with farm prices so low that farmers are faced with foreclosure—the farmer's burden is further increased by those who return from the city to seek relief and refuge on the land.

For the farmer—as for the businessman and worker in the city—this is another disheartening cycle of hope and despair which full employment would bring to an end.

WHAT FULL EMPLOYMENT MEANS
TO THE VETERAN

The veteran does not want a handout. He wants what all of the rest of his fellow citizens want—the opportunity to pursue a productive, profitable, and pleasurable life.

But, nonetheless, the veteran deserves special consideration. He deserves this not as a consequence of his military service—because such service is one of the obligations of citizenship. He deserves this special consideration because his service completely disrupted his pursuit of a normal career. Everyone in wartime, of course, experiences this disruption—but to a far less extent than the veteran.

Such preferential treatment, however, will give the returning serviceman hollow satisfaction—and only temporary security—unless he can work and live in a society and an economy that is sound and prosperous as a whole. It cannot be a question of one group of Americans profiting at the expense of another. We all must go forward or fall together. The ultimate problem of healthy re-employment for the veteran is the problem of full employment under an economy of abundance for *all* Americans able to work and wanting to work.

This does not, of course, remove the nation's special

obligation toward the veterans during the period of their transition from a world at war to a world at peace. There is no room here, nor is it my intention, to go into the individual psychological problem of war. But this much seems to me to be self-evident: the veteran comes back to us from another kind of world—one where individual action was limited in opportunity; where all his physical needs were automatically supplied, as far as the exigencies of combat permitted; where prolonged periods of restlessness, boredom, and frustration were broken by brief periods of intense and dangerous activity.

This is all very different from the usual routine of civilian life. The veteran, therefore, will very likely be an often-impatient and restless man—a man who very quickly can lose sight of the general public interest, and understandably so, if planning and action on the home front become delayed by prolonged debate and evasion of issues. The World War II veteran will have more decided ideas than the World War I veteran. This time the soldier or sailor has been longer in the service; he knows what happened after the last war; and he represents a much larger segment of our population than he did after World War I.

The returning veteran has every right to expect that, having gone all-out for war, we shall now go all-out to maintain the normal increases in our national production and thereby provide full employment. He has a right to demand that we make our political democracy function as a healthy economic democracy.

This is not a new demand in the history of our country. Let us look back a moment. After the Revolutionary War the returning soldiers ran into uncontrolled inflation and a flood of paper money. In western Massachusetts, conservative farmers were threatened with the loss of their homesteads through foreclosure. They rose in open revolt under Daniel Shays, an officer of the Continental Army, marched upon Springfield and took over the courts of law. This rebellion of American citizens had to be put down with Federal troops—and only after blood was shed was the situation mended and the currency stabilized.

After the Civil War the chance of similar trouble from dissatisfied citizens returning from the war was doubtless averted by building the Western railroads and opening homestead lands in the wilderness.

But after World War I, our general economic blundering brought on the mobilization of the Bonus Army and the March on Washington—ending with the miserable spectacle of the use of force against veterans who sought only peacetime jobs.

What will it be this time? We have the physical plant, the natural resources, and the tradition of boldness. If we fail in this we fail in the practical application of democracy. The only wilderness ahead of us today could be one of confused thinking, of timid or reactionary leadership. The land is ours in its fullness. We must plan together for its development. We must order its business to the uses of democracy.

Obviously we cannot promise the returning soldier or sailor or marine that he will step off his transport into a well-ordered and properly functioning postwar America— with a prearranged job all ready and waiting. He returns to his country as it faces a great task and a new challenge. Only one proposition will have been answered—namely, the barbarous master racist proposition that modern men cannot govern themselves but must be mechanized and chained to tyranny in order to survive. Our veterans provided the answer to that threat to our civilization.

But they come home to the new and more positive challenge—that a people can be continuously prosperous and productive in peace. The veteran has the right to demand this—but he also has the obligation to help prove it.

As for the nation's obligation to the veteran, the Congress already has made an acknowledgment of this in the statutes—in the job restoration provisions of the Selective Service Act and in the so-called "G.I. Bill of Rights." But as to the broadness and application of these statutes, controversies inevitably will arise.

Let me illustrate by a recent conversation with a top government official. He told me, "I have eighty-seven people employed in my immediate office—but there are ninety-three men who have gone from this office into the Armed Forces, and they are entitled to their jobs back under the G.I. Bill of Rights." I replied: "Your situation is simple compared with that in many businesses and industries." He immediately answered that the law was mandatory upon government while business and industry are allowed to take certain special situations into account.

The end result of this conversation is that it proved that the G.I. Bill of Rights doesn't mean much unless there is full employment for all. If there is not full employment, most of the veterans who borrow money to go into business will lose it; many of those who borrow money to buy farms will lose their farms; those who use the government to pay for their education may find it impossible to find a place for the specialized skill when they finish school. By all of which I mean to say that, fundamentally, the only real way to protect the veteran is to produce to the limit for a prosperous peace.

However, we do have the veteran's legislation on the statute books—and it is up to the Congress and the administrative agencies of government to make constant review of the legislation, its interpretation and application, so as to give quick relief where and when needed. But not all of the responsibility is up to the Federal or state governments. Much can and must be done in the veteran's own community.

Most communities long since have recognized their responsibility—and many already have put excellent plans into practice. For example, there is the smooth-functioning Community Advisory Service Center in Bridgeport, Connecticut, which has attracted nation-wide attention. Here, the veteran and displaced war worker are handled together—emphasizing the sameness of the problem.

This sameness was fully expressed in a statement made by Willard W. Rice, national service director of Disabled Veterans of America, in testifying before a Senate Committee. The veteran, he said, wants peace and security above all else. But he added:

"They will not find it in a mustering-out paycheck, a preferential rating for nonexistent jobs, or even in generous unemployment allowances. They will find it in the same way as their civilian neighbors—in an expanding economy that provides good jobs for all employables, not because they are veterans but because they are men."

Some fear that these initial aids and considerations for the veteran will create a semimilitary caste of millions of our young people—a caste or class that can be used by demagogues to intensify the class and racial divisions that are always latent in any society.

I have seen enough of our men in the armed services so that I do not share this fear. It would only be in the event of serious unemployment that our World War II veterans would respond to the demagogue.

Our people's army will want to return to the people from whence it sprang—to the farms, to industry, and to business. I am confident they will only seek to enjoy the rights and opportunities they fought to preserve. For our army is a responsible body of peace-loving young Americans. They can be made irresponsible only if we all, as a nation, are irresponsible—if we fail to meet the challenge of putting all of us to work.

PART THREE

The American Approach
to Abundance

I

The Framework of Freedom

SOME PEOPLE argue that we cannot meet this challenge of full employment within the framework—or, as they prefer to put it, the limits—of our capitalistic free-enterprise system. They want us to believe that full employment and free enterprise cannot flower together. They tell us that we cannot have full employment without inviting or forcing government to move in directly to control our economy—thereby, as they say, bringing about an end to our free-enterprise system. Shorn of the jargon of reaction, the argument of such people is plainly this—that participation by government to achieve the end of the general welfare is destructive of our national safety as a free people.

The premise of such an argument is untenable and the argument itself is fallacious.

Our capitalistic free-enterprise system was as revolutionary in its origin as our democratic political system. Both were born of rebellion against tyranny. And both have established a tradition of boldness in initiative and action. But down through the years, there has been too great a tendency to belittle the role of government—to subordinate, in the public minds, the political system to the economic. The nation was done a sad disservice when the teaching and practice of "economics"—as we know it today —became so far removed from "political economy."

From our very birth as a nation, the primary requirement in the relationship between the political and economic systems has been this—how to work out methods by which an ounce of government stimulation, or an ounce of government participation, would result in a pound of private initiative and enterprise.

In being guided by this formula, we have been following the line of action so wisely laid down by Alexander Hamilton—only down through the years, we have progressively applied this line of action to broaden the economic base for the benefit of the many, instead of limiting it to the privileged few as Hamilton always advocated.

In spite of the fact that in his day we were a newly formed and rapidly growing nation, Hamilton saw realistically the need for bolstering certain existing occupations with an ounce of government stimulation or participation so as to maintain the vigor of free enterprise. Only he called it the need for government "incitement and patronage." Hamilton also saw the necessity for helping reluctant venture capital over the initial obstacle of what we know today as the "abnormal risks" that our private financial institutions don't like to take. Only he called it a "degree of support from government" to overcome "the obstacles inseparable from first experiments." Today, we might say that this Hamiltonian prescription provides the vitamins of free enterprise.

I offer Alexander Hamilton's own words on these two points to those who may not be familiar with them, or may have forgotten them. The wisdom of these words will be as sound for our continued progress over the next 150 years as it has been during the past 150 years. This is the way Hamilton presented his economic prescription in his *Report on Manufactures,* in 1791:

Experience teaches, that men are often so much governed by what they are accustomed to see and practice, that the simplest and most obvious improvements, in the most ordinary occupations, are adopted with hesitation, reluctance, and by slow gradations. The spontaneous transition to new pursuits, in a community long habituated to different ones, may be expected to be attended with proportionately greater difficulty. When former occupations ceased to yield a profit adequate to the subsistence of their followers, or when there was an absolute deficiency of employment in them, owing to the superabundance of hands, changes would ensue; but these changes would be likely to be more tardy than might consist with the interest either of individuals or of society. In many cases they would not happen, while a bare support could be insured by an adherence to ancient courses, though a resort to a more profitable employment might be practicable. To produce the desirable changes as early as may be expedient may therefore require the incitement and patronage of government.

The apprehension of failing in new attempts is, perhaps, a more serious impediment. There are dispositions apt to be attracted by the mere novelty of an undertaking; but these are not always the best calculated to give it success. To this it is of importance that the confidence of cautious, sagacious capitalists, both citizens and foreigners, should be excited. And to inspire this description of persons with confidence, it is essential that they should be made to see in any project which is new—and for that reason alone, if for no other, precarious—the prospect of such a degree of countenance and support from government as may be capable of overcoming the obstacles inseparable from first experiments.

As for proof of the essential soundness of this belief of Hamilton's—which is, in short, that our democratic government has the definite responsibility of stimulating our free-enterprise system, not just in behalf of the general welfare, but also to keep free enterprise continuously a going concern—we need only to look at the record of our growth as a nation and as a people. The stimulating hand of government always helped us along the way.

Our westward progress, which symbolizes the dynamism of our growth as a nation, also symbolizes the role of the participation of government in our national development. For it was by such bold strokes as the Homestead Act and the subsidizing of the railroads, through both land grants and cash payments, that we built to the limit of our geographic frontiers.

Since then, this stimulation has been given in a variety of forms. For example, government participated in the expansion of the automobile industry by building more and better roads; and it shared similarly in the development of our shipping and aviation industries through the use of subsidy. With the inauguration of air mail, the government took all of the initial risk.

Largely because of this government stimulation and participation, we have never failed, even in the last three generations, to double our national production every twenty years. Today, we value our annual output of goods and services at over 200 billion dollars. If we live up to our past record of accomplishment—if we live up to our abilities to produce and our capacities to consume—then we shall measure our national production in the sixties at more than 300 billion dollars. But to do this we must shun those who preach the doctrines of scarcity—those who would seek safe profits by maintaining fat prices and lean levels of production, all at the expense of the unemployed. For this is monopoly in action—and monopoly always has been the worst enemy of free enterprise.

Thomas Jefferson sensed the threat of monopoly so keenly that he tried to place in the Bill of Rights of the Constitution a clause guaranteeing freedom from monopoly. The American people are well aware that there is no sin in bigness, itself. We have gloried in the efficiency of the industrial giants of mass production and mass distribution. But we also know, from the bitter and costly experiences of the past, that we must keep a sharp eye out for the monopolist. He is never too old to learn new tricks. He is still practicing and perfecting new tricks every day.

America is proud of its host of little men who have had big ideas. We shall continue to reward and honor those who apply their ingenuity to the multiplication of job opportunities. The key on the string of Benjamin Franklin's kite unlocked the door so that such men as Thomas Edison and Lee De Forest could lead us through it into the electronics age, with its limitless opportunities for service and employment. There were always others in all the other fields of enterprise—those whose big ideas created new industries upon which thousands of other business-men could build. And always, it has been American policy for government to encourage the little man to develop his ideas, and to oppose monopolistic agreements and unfair competition in trade.

The emergence of new industries after this war will keep open the American approach to the peace of abundance. This war has already given us striking advances in electronics, in transportation, in new synthetic products such as plastics, in light metals and new uses for steel. The armed forces have done a magnificent job in training technicians for these great industries of the future. And all of these developments can continue their breathless pace after the war—if the people desire it, and if they use their power to protect the new against the restraints of the old.

I fully expect that thirty years hence we shall be able to write the stories of the new Henry Fords of the 1970's in the same way that we write about the Ford of today. Henry Ford would have remained just a little man with an untried big idea if he had not succeeded in breaking the stranglehold of a patent cartel that would have made mass production of automobiles impossible. But Ford's greatest discovery was that the way to tap the common man's market was to raise wages and cut prices—meanwhile perfecting management and technological devices, so as to back up his daring innovations with solid competitive power.

Even though we have built to the limit of our geographical frontiers, we need have no fear that ours is a mature economy. The future is filled with new frontiers. And the most challenging of these is the human frontier. We must conquer the slums; we must rid ourselves of undernourishment; we must raise the general level of health; and we must make it possible for everyone to develop his or her latent capacities for work and profitable recreation. In doing these things we shall continue to multiply our job opportunities.

And beyond our physical borders lie new horizons abroad. The United States has assumed a long-awaited leadership in world co-operation. That means that we look east to Europe for the opportunity to assist in restoring war-torn countries; we look west across the Pacific to aid in the industrialization of Asia; and we look south to fruitful co-operation with the Latin American republics, where a total population somewhat larger than that of the United States is eager to use our industries, our skills and technical know-how, in raising its living standards.

But to build to the limits of these new frontiers, we must first make certain that we organize our democratic processes in such a way as to keep free enterprise not only free, but functioning on a continuing basis. To do this, we need to re-examine the position and responsibilities of all groups in our national life, private and public. In short, we must put our self-governing machinery in the best possible state of repair to serve the welfare of all.

II

Keeping Free Enterprise Free

WHAT SHOULD be the role of government in promoting the general welfare? For many years I have been seeking an equitable answer to this most essential of all questions—an answer equitable to all of us. And I have sought the answer from leaders in government, from leaders in academic life, and from leaders in labor, agriculture, and business management.

In concluding the Weil Lectures on American Citizenship at the University of North Carolina, in the spring of 1937, I raised the question thus:

Is it now conceded that the function of government is somewhat more than that of an economic salvage crew? Is the cost of salvage, of cleaning up the wreckage from boom and depression, now so great that government should be asked to prevent some of the destruction from ever occurring? If the answer to these questions is "Yes," then of course government must exert an integrating and stabilizing influence in our economy.

Corporations, labor unions, and farm organizations are continually making decisions which affect both production and prices. Many of the decisions made by corporations, labor unions and farm organizations are made with the knowledge or actual help of the government. More and more the government is being made aware of the way its monetary policies, tariff policies, regulatory activities, and Federal expenditures affect the general welfare. A new science of government is in the making, the broad outlines of which are just beginning to appear.

There is a tendency for organized groups to believe that by exerting pressure they can get from society more than is there. They have had enough temporary success with the use of pressure to be encouraged in this belief. . . .

It is perfectly true that any one group can, for a time, get a larger share of the national income, but it doesn't work when all try it at the same time. Sooner or later the pressure game will blow up in our faces unless we provide a constantly larger national income to divide up. This is really a matter of simple but intensely practical arithmetic. Unless we learn it, our future is black indeed.

If government is to be partly a policeman, partly a coordinator, partly a clearinghouse, and partly a stimulator—all on behalf of the general welfare—the problem of economic democracy becomes supremely important. If government marches into the economic field decisively and directly at the top, the result can be a regimentation of all types of activity in a manner completely abhorrent to the American temperament. . . .

Economic democracy means that the various economic groups must have equality of bargaining power. But going along with this *right*, there is also the *duty* of serving the general welfare.

Fundamentally, the most significant things in a modern economy are ideas, technology, and natural resources. Secondary to these are the corporations, the co-operatives, the labor unions, the farm organizations, and other organizations through which a true economic democracy can express itself. Here in the United States, at the moment, we have by far the best opportunity to work out an economic democracy which can serve as a model for the entire world. The new world of the general welfare is beckoning. New opportunities await the men with a bent for public service, whether in government, in labor, or in management. The rewards in terms of satisfaction are far beyond those which any captain of industry in the nineteenth century could dream of. The world to which I refer is not fanciful or unreal. The foundation is now being laid, and it is to be hoped that no disturbance abroad will distract our attention from the real job here at home.

To say simply that disturbance and distraction did come upon us would be, of course, a gross understatement. Once the first Nazi Panzer division pierced the Polish frontiers, our involvement in World War II was inevitable. Our people saw that government not only had to move in decisively and directly at the top; it also had to reach down to the bottom to see to it that the country was mobilized for all-out production so that we and our Allies could survive as nations. Now, secure in the world again, we take up once more the promotion of the general welfare in peace—and first, we must find new and democratic ways to meet the problems that peace will bring.

First, though, we must spend some time in the classroom of our experiences and profit from some hard-learned lessons. For just as in equipping ourselves for World War

If we benefited from our experiences in World War I—so can we profit, in finding answers to the postwar problems ahead of us, by paying attention to what happened after the last war as to both immediate and long-term problems. Then we will be better equipped to make our advances in the science of democratic government.

The most important decision facing the nation right now is that of responsibility for maintaining employment and prosperity, and the longer we postpone the decision, the graver will be the consequences of the delay. Most people, I am sure, believe that this responsibility must be placed with, and exercised by, their national government. But that belief has not yet been reflected in positive legislative action. Government takes the brunt of the blame when things go wrong economically—but it has never been clearly entrusted with the responsibility for keeping them right. If government is to co-operate effectively with business, labor, and agricultural groups in establishing and maintaining peacetime prosperity, the people of this country, speaking through their elected representatives in Congress, must write that responsibility into law.

Our Federal government today in both the executive and legislative branches is so much a reflection of the "pressure groups" that we can't expect any truly unified governmental policy with regard to reconversions, taxes, tariffs, and full employment itself, unless these great private groups can agree as to the demands of the peace and general welfare. In assigning responsibility to government, then, the people should also make it plain that they expect these groups to co-operate continuously, among themselves

79

and with their government, to arrive at the maximum in unified policy.

Only by doing these things right now can the people avoid another rush back to an irresponsible "normalcy."

IT WAS NO ONE'S RESPONSIBILITY LAST TIME

In the first year after World War I we had perhaps the wildest commodity price inflation this country has ever seen. This broke in the summer of 1920, and downward we slid, reaching the depth of this depression in the fall of 1921. We finally succeeded in leveling upward again into several years of full employment and great superficial prosperity in the cities. This was based on the following four factors:

1. The housing boom;
2. A huge government road building program;
3. A great expansion in the automobile and the radio industry;
4. A vigorous export trade fostered by government and supported by loans abroad.

The building boom, the expansion in the automobile industry, and the export trade all reached their greatest proportions during the period from 1925 to 1929. Those were the days when thousands of people felt they had found the road to easy wealth by following the magic path of speculation. Neither the leaders of government nor those of business felt that anything needed to be done to assure continuing prosperity and employment. Leave Things Alone! Don't Disturb Business Confidence! Don't

Sell America Short! These were the high-pressure watchwords we heard daily as our leaders assured us we were moving effortlessly, and as if by magic, to higher plateaus of permanent prosperity.

Even if any leader of government had dared to tell the truth then, he would have been blamed for causing the very thing which finally happened. The truth was that this wondrous prosperity rested more upon a speculative boom than upon the production of more goods and services for more and more people. We had developed a huge export market on the basis of loans made abroad—many of these loans having been made on an unsound basis. And then we had raised our tariffs, making it more difficult for other nations to sell us their products to get the money wherewith to repay their loans. By expanding private bank credit we had greatly increased the potential consumer purchasing power in the United States—far too much of the money went into the stock market. Even the housing boom failed miserably to meet the basic need of more decent housing at low prices. Scant consideration was given to maximum service to the purchaser. Rather, housing was more of a racket whereby several groups combined to hold up prices so high as to make it almost impossible for the average home-seeker to get a decent house at a price he could afford. Certainly we cannot be very proud of our housing record after World War I.

Indeed, our whole economic structure in those years was built on the sands of speculation—and when the floods came and the winds blew the structure fell. The whole world was shaken by that fall.

The 100-billion-dollar purchasing power which the people of the United States enjoyed in 1929 shrank in three years to 50 billion. No other nation has ever gone through such a great melting away of prosperity in such a short period of time. That was the cost of our mad, planless rush back to "normalcy" after World War I.

WE FACE THE SAME DANGERS THIS TIME

As I look ahead at the coming postwar period, I find many elements almost identical with those that existed after World War I. It would be so easy to have another soaring inflation, say in 1946 or 1947—followed by a sudden sharp smash in prices in 1947 or 1948. It would be so easy after these first difficulties have been corrected to level out, in the fifties, with several years of prosperity based on a housing boom, large sales of automobiles, radios, and refrigerators, large industrial exports based on credits, as well as greatly increased activity in the building of airports and airplanes for private flying. But I can also see this boom blowing up in the early fifties for the same reasons as in the late twenties—with the certainty of a subsequent depression far more serious.

To offset this gloomy possibility, we have the fact that the leaders in government, business, labor, and agriculture have all learned a lot as a result of their experiences after the last war. I would cite particularly the work of the Committee for Economic Development, composed entirely of businessmen; and the National Planning Association, composed of leaders in business, labor, and agriculture. These organizations have done a thorough job of surveying such postwar problems as full employment, reconversion, fiscal policy, and public works. As a result of the thoughtful leadership furnished by these and other private agencies, the "pressure groups" are better equipped than ever before with the factual basis for making decisions—both as how best to prevent a recurrence of the ruinous inflation-deflation cycle and to plan intelligently for the full use of all our resources.

Opposed to the constructive attitude of these private agencies, there is a loud but limited group that seemingly believes it is the devil's own sin to make any plans whatsoever. These people tell us that all planning is just plain Hitlerian tyranny. They profess to make no distinction at all between the absolute planned social-economic life of the regimented state—or Planned Economy, as we perhaps know it best—and democratic planning to preserve our free enterprise system and our free way of life from the very dangers of totalitarianism that are inherent in inaction.

I have always tried to be tolerant and appreciative of honest differences of viewpoint and opinion—but at the same time I have never been able to shirk plain speech. And to me, those who spread such beliefs—whether they are conscious evildoers or just unwitting dupes—are spreading the seeds of our destruction as a free people. They are doing the spadework for the fanatics and bigots who would kill off all that is fine and decent and godlike in our free institutions. They are, whether they realize it or not, serving those who wrap themselves with the flag of patriotism and do the dirty work of scoundrels.

THEY KNOW WHAT'S WHAT AT THE GRASS ROOTS

Fortunately, I do not believe that these agents of the wretched life have much of a following as yet. In recent months, I have made a special effort to acquaint myself with what was going on at the grass roots. I wanted to find out just what people were thinking about and talking about—yes, and planning about—along Main Street. And I have been greatly encouraged.

Shortly after I became Secretary of Commerce, a boyhood friend of mine who is now Executive Secretary of the Chamber of Commerce of Albert Lea, in Minnesota, sent me a prospectus of that city's own community development agency known as "Jobs, Incorporated"—a nonprofit corporation with a subscription capital of $100,000 for use in developing new local job opportunities by starting new local industries. One sentence from this Albert Lea prospectus forcibly strikes me as applicable to all communities. It reads: "There can be no economic security unless the citizens of each community recognize their responsibility to create jobs." Surely, this is the sum total of community responsibility everywhere.

Upon my desk there have been piled higher and higher the earnest, painstaking plans of communities and states —and as I have pored through them I have come to know that Main Street was not waiting for either Wall Street or Pennsylvania Avenue.

Picking at random from these plans, there is the splendid job done by a city in South Carolina. It's entitled

84

"Anderson—After the War." And it is an imaginative and complete job of examining and charting local problems —even down to anticipated expenditures for housing and automobiles and new farm equipment in the immediate postwar years.

Another of these booklets leads off with the question— "Why Plan?" And there follows—"Because it will be a tough job to change over from war to peace without wrecking the state." This one comes from the Arkansas Economic Council. And the bolder letters on the cover read, "Action—Arkansas." Another excellent survey, that of Fort Smith in Arkansas, bears the title: "Fort Smith— Forward by Plan."

I have read through the pile of such booklets at hand— and I am certain the pile will keep getting higher. And I have learned that planning has become firmly entwined with the grass roots. I have come to know that the people, themselves, profess no fears of democratic planning. Back on Main Street, they know what they want—they want action. And they appreciate, I am certain, this basic fact —that to win the peace of abundance within the framework of free enterprise requires even more planning than was required to win the war. This does not mean that the wartime powers of the President must be perpetuated into the peace—but it does mean that the President and the Congress must be given the responsibility for prompter, more decisive, more comprehensive action than was ever required of them before in a time of peace.

We, as a free people, will never tolerate government as a bureaucratic monopolist—any more than we shall ever tolerate the monopolistic controls of industrial or financial giants. But we do not need to fear any monopoly of planning in Washington so long as there is such an alert public opinion at the grass roots.

THE NATION'S MOST DECISIVE PLANNING

As we approach this problem of the most difficult peace the world has ever faced, it is well for us to take counsel from our great forefathers. At a time when they were confronted with chaos, they, too, were forced to debate the fundamental governmental problem of reconciling the maximum of liberty with the necessary unity. Our Constitution is the embodiment of that debate. We almost had anarchy in the United States in 1785 for the same reason that there is trouble in so many of the liberated countries in Europe today. We had fought against tyranny and therefore our people felt that any type of central government was likely to develop into a tyrant.

But the great men of that day, after their experience with the weak government under the Articles of Confederation, recognized that central government must be given certain responsibilities having to do with taxation, tariffs, the coining of money, the running of an army and making of laws. They recognized that these responsibilities must be assigned to government by the people in order to prevent liberty from degenerating into license and anarchy. And it is one of the miracles of all time that our forefathers, living when more than 90 per cent of the United States was agricultural, could have devised a constitution which would apply so well to a highly industrial civilization.

This document will receive its greatest trial in the years immediately ahead. But if we apply the constitutional authority in the same spirit in which our forefathers devised it, we need have no fear as to our ability to reconcile energetic, decentralized liberty in certain fields with orderly, centralized unity in others.

As we consider the mistakes which we made after World War I, and as we contemplate the terrific magnitude of the forces descending upon us as a result of World War II, we can easily recognize that our problem is not one of changing the general framework of government. The problem is one of policy with regard to exercising wisely the economic powers that are already vested in the Federal government. The problem is to use the same spirit which the founders used, not to change the constitutional authority, but to develop under the Constitution new mechanisms to enable us to meet economic problems in a wise and orderly way. The need for making this decision was not forced on us until we became a highly industrialized creditor nation. Now we can no longer escape it without injustice and tragedy both to ourselves and to the world.

Our problem, in brief, is for Americans to organize the activities of the Federal government in taxation, agricultural adjustment, social security, foreign trade, resource development, and other fields so as continuously to promote in private enterprise the maximum of sound employment and business activity. We must do this to keep free enterprise free and functioning continuously. For this is the essential process of our own freedom.

I am sure that 90 per cent of the people want government to help create the basic conditions for full employment. I am sure that just as they called upon government to clean up the economic mess of 1929–1932, so now they expect government to give centralized direction to the job of preventing another one in 1952. There are a few, of course, who think that any government servant who uses the phrases "full employment" or "60 million jobs" is engaged in some dark, deep plot. But they are the exceptions that prove the people's sanity and soundness as a whole.

The people know well that we have already created for ourselves a number of basic conditions for full employment without in the least departing from our democratic traditions. We now have a social-security program covering 34 millions of people, or about 90 per cent of all persons working outside of government, farming, or domestic service. Moreover, the Congress is now considering the extension of social security to all the people.

Without losing our liberties, we have firmly established collective bargaining as an essential principle of economic democracy; and we have given the worker a guarantee as to his minimum wage and maximum hours of work. And here again, there is Congressional consideration under way to lift the minimum—to make better customers of those who have been making less than $1000 a year.

Similarly, we have put a floor under farm income by providing that farm prices for two years after the war will be held close to parity levels, meaning a level comparable with prices of city goods. And for certain basic crops, we have provided crop insurance against natural hazards.

We have given the government responsibility for keeping credit at low rates—thereby stimulating employment, particularly in the construction of homes, factories, and warehouses, and in the public-utilities industry.

We have given these and other stimulants to full employment without losing any of our freedom. We have been able to do this because it is the genius of democracy to seek continually the proper balance between absolute liberty and absolute control and to find it at the point where the minimum measure of control will give us the maximum of liberty.

Fifteen years ago a famous German agricultural economist visited me in Des Moines, and I asked him what impressed him most about the United States. He replied: "The extraordinary discipline which you Americans display in observing so precisely the green and red lights of your traffic signals." In other words, this student of social and economic organization saw in the daily activity of the millions of American automobile drivers the proper balance between liberty and control so that all of them could live together happily on the road.

That is our job today—to find the mechanism, properly balanced between liberty and control, for stimulating full employment and keeping free enterprise free. We can do this if we approach the problem in the same spirit with which our founders approached the decision on the Constitution. And in doing it we shall be making an *economic* discovery which will deserve to rank with our Constitution as a *political* discovery.

"Jobs and Opportunities for All"

Both Franklin Roosevelt and Thomas E. Dewey expressed themselves about this problem in much the same terms. In his last budget message to Congress, in January of 1945, President Roosevelt said:

"It is the responsibility of business enterprise to translate market opportunities into employment and production. It is the responsibility of government to hold open the door of opportunity and to assure sustained markets. Then, and then only, can free enterprise provide jobs."

Governor Dewey said almost identically the same thing while he was campaigning for the presidency during the fall of 1944:

"Government's first job in the peacetime years ahead will be to see that conditions exist which promote widespread job opportunities in private enterprise. If at any time there are not sufficient jobs in private employment to go around, the government can and must create job opportunities because there must be jobs for all in this country of ours—

"We in this country must have jobs and opportunities for all. That is everybody's business. Therefore, it is the business of government."

The economic climate in the United States today is greatly different from what it was twenty-seven years ago among both Republicans and Democrats, among both businessmen and workers. The statements by the late President and Governor Dewey reflect the strong feeling on the part of the public that great danger lies ahead. They prove that the public knows that neither business alone nor labor, nor agriculture, nor bankers, nor government can prevent a serious postwar inflation followed by depression. The people want united action.

In order that all of us may work together to do the job, government must be definitely assigned its full peacetime responsibility, and must carry out that responsibility. This peacetime responsibility under the thesis set forth by both President Roosevelt and Governor Dewey would be to see to it that the total of job-creating expenditures from all sources—business, consumers, and government—should add up to enough year after year to provide full employment. My interpretation of the responsibility of government is that in the early postwar years, action should be taken to check the decline in employment, by stimulating opportunities for business activity and the demand for workers in private industry—and government should be authorized to initiate its own supplementary programs if such stimulation fails to do the whole job.

No statement of desirable government policy standing by itself will convince an individualistic American businessman that something is going to happen. Government must be made responsible for definite action; it must be organized to do its job. The nation wants to make sure that the largest possible number of jobs will be provided through private business. And in working to this end, the first obligation of government, therefore, will be to explore all possible actions that can be taken to enlarge this private demand, then to find out how big the markets will be for the products of private industry—and finally to supplement that demand, if necessary, with productive public activity.

In the final analysis, the voter is the government. It is the voter who is responsible for full employment; therefore, he wants to be in a position to call his President and his Congress promptly to account. But the voter needs organization in order that he may tell them what results he wants them to produce—he needs organization to know just what his President and his Congress are doing to carry out his orders.

I believe, therefore, that the President should be directed by law to submit to Congress a national full-employment budget each year. The voter would be able to check first on his President and second on his Congress as to how well they were carrying out their responsibilities. The President and the Congress would have to work together more than ever before in considering the economic situation of the entire nation. And when this same responsibility is expanded to bring in state and city governments, then we shall be able to benefit to the fullest possible extent from the community planning at the grass roots.

This local participation is especially needed when it comes to housing, health, and public works of any kind. When it comes to roads and certain types of airports, however, state and national considerations cannot be forgotten. All we ask in a democracy is a practical reconciliation between the national and the local point of view; between liberty and unity—so that the happiness of the individual and the security of the nation may be preserved.

COMPETITION THROUGH PLANNING

Those who in recent months have been talking most vigorously against planning of any kind also tell us that planning might somehow be all right if only it did not lead to a reduction in competition. This is economic double-talk. The planning involved in drawing up a national full-employment budget would lead to more competition rather than less. It would lead to less inflation, less deflation, and less speculation. The average businessman would have a better chance.

If free enterprise meant recurring swings from one million to 20 million men unemployed, then free enterprise as we have known it would not last long. But free enterprise, instead, can be made a system which enables the ordinary farmer and the average businessman to go ahead producing abundantly year after year without fear of bankruptcy—while at the same time the worker can go ahead year after year without fear of not being able to find a good job. Free enterprise stands a much better chance of keeping the vigor of youth if the people provide that government shall take forethought by means of periodic national budgets, and shall act appropriately in plenty of time.

The national budget to promote full employment will make it possible for government to organize on a businesslike basis those activities that the people want it to carry on continuously year in and year out—and to prepare, and keep in readiness, the proper short-term programs for emergencies. Certainly I cannot agree that this kind of

93

planning will interfere with free competition. I say that it will make for the healthiest kind of competition—namely, competition in productivity rather than competition in freebooting.

PART FOUR

New Frontiers of Abundance

I

The Backlog of Abundance

WHENEVER THE Dow-Jones ticker, in prewar days, carried the news of a new high for the year in the backlog of some industrial giant—say, "Big Steel"—there was an immediate response of enthusiasm and increased confidence in the financial district. The more unfilled orders on the books, the healthier were the times.

In wartime, there is no concern over backlogs. The Federal government, with its huge appropriations and its tremendous needs, simply tells business to get going. With these firm orders on hand business then proceeds to perform its miracles of wartime production.

For business, whether in peace or war, there is no greater driving power than plenty of unfilled orders on the books to keep production at a high level. Every businessman knows that then he can easily manage his other problems. He can deal liberally with labor, set his prices in line with volume and costs, and continue to search for more efficient ways of doing the job.

The volume of war orders is shrinking rapidly—and we must look elsewhere quickly and decisively, to build up the backlogs to give us the driving power for peace.

We do, of course, build up an equivalent to backlogs in

wartime. For the immediate reconversion period, we have the enormous pent-up demand for the consumer goods the people were unable to buy in the war years—and the necessity of replacing worn-out plant and machinery. This demand now becomes the backlog of unfilled orders for business—and this will give business its initial driving power.

Almost everything the consumers own—automobiles, tires, radios, furniture, shoes, refrigerators, the closet full of clothes—is badly depreciated, if not worn out, as a result of wartime scarcities. On a conservative basis, the automobile industry, for example, would have to produce from 6 to 8 million passenger cars a year for four or five years just to catch up with the accumulated demand at home and abroad. Shelves and warehouses everywhere must be stocked anew with everything from hairpins to sheets, from baseball bats to musical instruments.

The business backlog not only includes replacements of worn-out plant and machinery, but also provides the additional capacity needed to expand our civilian industries to full employment dimensions. This expansion will be exceptionally marked in industries that had little expansion during the war—such as clothing, textiles, shoes, paper goods and publishing, recreation, building materials, and the service industries generally.

But to maintain the national initiative, we must think about backlogs in broader and longer terms. We must become enthusiastic not just about the backlogs of unfilled orders in business, but also about backlogs for the nation as a whole—the government's backlogs of productive work to supplement and stimulate business and industry. For this is the people's backlog of unfinished national business —the backlog of the new frontiers of abundance.

The items in this list include our need for more houses than ever before, more hospitals, more schools, more rural electrification, more soil conservation, more river-valley developments, more and better transportation facilities, more industrialization in the South and other regions where people normally are underemployed and don't produce enough—and finally, more international co-operation to help build up the undeveloped human and natural resources of other lands. These are some of the people's unfilled orders that must go onto the books of the nation. They represent millions of jobs and work to be done everywhere that needs only the touch of government encouragement and stimulation to release the driving power of private enterprise. These are the opportunities which show us the shape of things to come—the future that is ours if we are big enough to meet the challenge.

OUR FRONTIER OF HOUSING

Housing is probably the largest of our new frontiers of job opportunities. Franklin Roosevelt in 1937 told us that one third of the nation was ill-housed. We now know that nearly half of our homes are below minimum standards. And we know, too, that slum conditions exist to greater or less extent in every city and town in the land. Correction of this situation will provide work enough to keep several million persons busy for at least ten years.

There are many reasons why housing holds so prominent a place in any program of full employment

The first reason is simply the greatness of the need. Every family with any sense of responsibility wants a good home, near a good school, in which to bring up healthy children in decency. Yet according to the 1940 census, nearly one fourth of the 37 million dwelling units in the country needed major repairs, the continued neglect of which threatens the safety of the residents, while another one fourth were in need of plumbing, heating, or other primary essentials to decent living.

If these needs were to be met over a ten-year period, it would require the construction of from 16 to 18 million new units, and improvements in from 9 to 10 million existing units. The new units would consist of:

8 to 9 million dwelling units to replace those that have already outlived their usefulness.

3 million dwelling units to replace those that will become dilapidated during the ten-year period.

5 to 6 million additional housing units to meet the demand from increased population and new families.

This is the job before us. Some will say that this is setting our goals too high. And the very ones who say there will not be jobs enough for 60 million people by 1950 will be the first to point out that 2 million housing units per year are more than twice the number built in any previous year. But the exact number of units is not important at this stage. What does matter is that we make our plans fit our needs. And I don't think the country will be reaching for the moon if it aims at such a housing goal—for even this program will supply all of us with only minimum, not with maximum, standards. These minimum standards include, in either house or apartment, only these primary essentials: adequate light and air, enough space for privacy —about one room per person—weatherproof walls and roof, inside running water, bath or shower and an indoor toilet; heating facilities (fireplace or stove) where the climate demands; refrigeration of some sort; and electricity where feasible. Surely, there is little here of the "dream house" of the postwar electronics age. These are only the bare essentials which merit constant repetition because so many in the upper half of our population actually do not fully realize what an important role proper housing plays in the physical and social well-being of the nation; they do not fully realize how much less juvenile delinquency, disease, and crime there is in modern housing projects compared with conditions in adjoining slum areas.

The second reason why better housing and full employment are inseparable is that we cannot meet our housing needs without continuous full employment. To build to the minimum standard calls for an annual expenditure of about 8 billion dollars—and if we allow for the cost of needed repairs for existing substandard homes, the annual expenditure for housing would exceed 9 billion dollars. To spend that much on housing, the nation must be fully employed—and government must exercise some responsibility for helping low-income families obtain decent homes. About a third of the housing need embraces families who cannot afford more than a 30-dollar rental per month. Another third can afford only from $30 to $50 per month. Everyone knows that we can't get the needed volume of units to rent for less than $30 per month without some government-aid subsidy—at least where abnormal risks exist.

It is in the other two thirds of the housing market, where rentals run from $30 to $50 and over, that we find the best opportunity for expansion by private enterprise, either on its own or with some government stimulation. In recent years, public-housing activity has been concerned chiefly with the lower-rental need, while private construction activity has concentrated on meeting the demand of the upper-income brackets—leaving too largely neglected the needs of the middle-income groups. In the postwar building cycle, there is a joint obligation of government and private housing interests to make sure that the needs of all groups are met.

A third reason for considering housing in relation to full employment is that the contribution of housing to full employment can be so very substantial. In sustained full employment, housing can provide both directly and indirectly at least 4 million jobs. To build the 16 to 18 million new units over a ten-year period would require the full time of about 3 million men a year both on-site and off-site for ten years. Off-site workers would include those in industries that supply the building trades—in brickyards, in quarries, in manufacturing plants of all kinds. Another 200,000 men or so would be needed full time to bring substandard units up to the minimum—making a total of about 3,200,000 jobs merely to provide a minimum standard of housing for the nation.

But this would not be the total employment in housing. In addition there will be many thousands of carpenters, bricklayers, painters, electricians, and plumbers employed in the ordinary routine of building and remodeling for those who can afford the luxury of more than a minimum-standard home.

The fourth reason why housing and full employment are so essential to each other has to do with getting a more nearly even balance in our economy. The jerry-built housing booms of the past have helped to build full employment on a foundation of quicksand; when the booms broke, the subsequent stagnation in housing then held back our recovery. The record of our home-building activity over the past 150 years reminds one of the ebb and flow of a heavy tide. Approximately every eighteen years we have experienced the hustle and bustle of a building boom —followed by prolonged stagnation and broken hopes.

The backlog demand for housing created in recent years, and largely left unsatisfied because of the war, means that we are definitely headed for another boom. If this demand, under the impetus of spending wartime savings, is allowed to develop without regard to the construction costs—and without regard to unified planning in cities and communities—we shall merely boom and go broke as before. Based on past patterns, we would in a very short while reach a yearly total of 900,000 units, and then quickly subside to about 100,000 units per year—without having made any real progress in meeting the housing needs of the low-income groups in the cities, villages, and rural areas.

Our final reason for combining our interest in housing with our interest in full employment is that we cannot look forward to the necessary doubling of our past performance—and have the units evenly distributed to meet the needs of all income groups, and the construction evenly distributed over the years to steady our economy—without doing something about the long-recognized afflictions of the housing industry. It suffers from too-high distribution costs and from ineffective selling methods; from high labor costs which nevertheless do not provide adequate wages the year around; and from a multiplicity of other ailments, including the improper building codes and application of agreements between employers and unions in the building trades which restrict the volume of construction. The importance of this industry to full employment is so great that responsible management and labor in the industry must explore these drawbacks thoroughly and expeditiously, and co-operate with government—Federal, state, and local—to bring about their removal.

There is almost universal recognition that long-range planning of housing construction is necessary to attain greater stability in all of the construction industry. Housing not only represents a very large part of all construction, but is chiefly responsible for the great swings in total construction employment. Our aim, therefore, should be to make unified plans for the whole of the construction industry so as to maintain total construction at an adequate and gradually expanding level. This would make construction the stabilizer for a national economy of full employment, just as the spine gives form and stability to the human body.

Prior to the war, the Federal government's interest in

housing was divided among several agencies. But the President used his wartime powers to consolidate all housing functions under the National Housing Agency. This consolidation should be made permanent by the Congress in order to enable the government to function at a maximum of efficiency in handling postwar housing expansion. This would make it possible for the housing industry and other interested bodies to co-operate more effectively with government. Men and women who know their job in housing and city planning, both in and out of government, have laid excellent foundations for us to build on—not only to meet the need for decent homes for the poorer half of our population, but also to promote full-scale urban development. Under a consolidated government housing agency, we shall have a much better chance of finishing the job.

But government participation in making available all the fiscal planning and research aids at its disposal should not obscure the basic working principle that housing is essentially a community endeavor and cannot be provided by Washington. The role of the Federal government must be subordinate to that of the community. Here, as elsewhere, the government can accomplish what the nation wants by applying an ounce of stimulus where necessary to get the maximum of community or private enterprise.

OUR FRONTIER OF HEALTH

Sickness and disability in the United States cost us some 2 million man-years of working time every year, or more than 5 billion dollars. Every year the nation's total bill for sickness and postponable death is over 10 billion dollars.

Forty out of every hundred Americans examined for military duty were physically or mentally unfit.

We cannot long afford this colossal waste—not when we must make the fullest use of *all* our resources, including manpower, if we are to keep pace with the demands for development not only in this country but throughout the world.

Certainly we have brought about great improvements in the national health since the days of the Revolution. We have raised the average man's life expectancy from 35 to 64 years. We have made great advances in saving babies and mothers, and preventing epidemics. In most of our cities we have built safe water systems, good sewage-disposal facilities, and other sanitary systems.

But we have made astonishingly little progress toward the democratic idea of "health-plus" for all the people. Our health record is particularly bad in the low-income groups. The lower a man's income, the poorer his health and that of his children, and therefore the greater their chances for an earlier death. Health standards among Negroes have improved faster during the past fifty years than among whites. But the Negro's life expectancy today still is only equal to that of the white man twenty-five years ago. With further improvement in the incomes and living standards of these low-earning groups, I would expect health conditions among them to improve markedly.

Poverty and sickness form a vicious circle. Each links with the other to affect mind and body. More than half the hospital beds in the country are occupied by mentally ill persons whose illness in many cases is directly traceable to lack of jobs or to inadequate income.

Recent statistics, made available from Selective Service examinations and other sources, have shown us that great numbers of the American people are improperly fed. Of course, this means not only that they must have correct information about what kinds of food they need to eat in order to remain healthy; it also means that there must be full employment, and wages high enough to permit families to buy the food they need to build up and maintain their health. To the extent that we provide steady jobs for all, at decent wages, we shall be striking at much of the waste caused by sickness and early death.

But this is far from being the whole cure. We must strike also at inadequate supplies of hospitals and doctors and their inaccessibility to whole sections of the population. Shortly before the war a Federal interdepartmental committee of experts reported to the President that:

Services to prevent sickness are grossly inadequate for the nation as a whole.

Hospitals and other needed institutions to cure illness are much too few, especially in rural areas; the financial support of such institutions is shaky and inadequate.

One third of our population receives either no medical care at all or completely inadequate care.

A much larger number suffer from the economic burdens caused by illness.

These conditions have been heightened by the war, and they will continue long after peace comes, unless we take definite remedial action now.

We must build more public-health facilities and more hospitals, and we must have the professional staffs to man them. We must make sure that people everywhere have access to these facilities whenever and wherever they need them, no matter what their means. And we must find some way to meet the costs of sickness without dragging whole families down into poverty and despair.

The best way to conquer sickness is to prevent it. This is why we need a greatly expanded public-health service. We need this expansion to safeguard water and milk supplies better, and to control communicable diseases for an ever-expanding population. We need it to intensify the fight against infant mortality; to promote industrial hygiene and mental health and provide diagnostic services and serums on an ever-increasing basis. And with this expanded public-health program we can wipe out venereal disease, tuberculosis, and typhoid completely in the postwar generation.

Today, only about 1850 of our more than 3000 counties have any organized public-health service. Most of these are inadequate. The first of our postwar responsibilities in health, therefore, must be to spread good public-health service throughout *all* the country.

But about three fourths of the illnesses and deaths which occur today are due to chronic diseases, which cannot be eliminated by public-health measures. The only way to control them is through early diagnosis and proper care. And this is expensive. Furthermore, chronic diseases occur twice as frequently among people of low income as among those in the middle- and higher-income brackets.

To check and cure chronic diseases we must depend upon an adequate supply of hospitals and doctors. In 1940, there were around 1200 counties containing more than 15 million people which had no hospitals at all, although some of these got a little service from adjoining areas. A great many other counties have only the poorest facilities. The number of hospital beds in a poorer region, moreover, is much smaller in relation to the population than in richer sections. Modern doctors are reluctant to set up practice where good hospital facilities are either nonexistent or insufficient. Consequently, whole areas of the nation suffer from shortages of both good physicians and hospital facilities.

The second of our immediate postwar needs in health, then, is a nationwide hospital-construction program.

Surgeon General Thomas Parran of the United States Public Health Service estimates that the nation needs the following new hospital facilities and replacements:

166,000 beds for general hospitals

191,000 beds for hospitals for **nervous and mental dis**eases

44,000 beds for tuberculosis hospitals

And here again, just as with housing and education, we must realize that not only would we be providing additional hospitals to improve the efficiency of *all* the people, but we would be creating more jobs. Not only would we be raising the nation's health—we would be helping the whole of our economy.

But building more hospitals and expanding public-health services does not solve all our problems. We must find a way to meet the costs of medical care in serious or prolonged illness. If illness can easily consume all of the savings of a family in comfortable circumstances and put them into debt, what chance has a family in the low-income group?

While the costs of medical care for any one individual family are unpredictable and often financially disastrous, they can be quite accurately calculated for the whole nation and apportioned on a family or individual basis. Thus apportioned, each family's share in the total cost is small enough to be met with far less difficulty than even one serious illness. This program of sharing by all in the cost of medical care—which we know as health insurance—has long been advocated as an essential part of the general social-insurance program of the nation.

Most people are familiar with voluntary health-insurance organizations, which provide hospital and other medical services for a small regular payment. These voluntary arrangements are excellent—but only a few million persons in the United States actually have such medical and hospital insurance. Unfortunately, most people just don't think about protecting themselves against sickness until it is too late. Or they feel that they can't afford it, or perhaps only the head of the family is covered. The average wage earner is not going to be able to afford such insurance until the cost is spread over the whole population so that each individual pays only a very small amount.

Our program to secure for everyone the "health-plus" which our modern science and our national resources make possible should be the following:

Steady work in healthful surroundings, at wages that support a decent diet and healthful standard of living.

Adequate public-health service everywhere.

Good hospital, laboratory, and medical services accessible to *everyone*.

Adequate publicly supported medical care for the needy. Health insurance under which each person contributes his share toward supporting public facilities, and takes out insurance to pay for medical and hospital care when needed.

Fair compensation to the individuals and agencies which furnish health and medical services.

Adequate support of research to maintain and improve the quality of service and extend the boundaries of scientific skill and knowledge.

Assuring such medical and hospital care to everyone is more important even than building roads, constructing dams, or saving soil. No price is too high to pay for a healthy, vigorous and productive people.

The first cost of the hospital construction and facilities we need would be about 2 billion dollars, according to the estimates of Surgeon General Parran. It would take about a million man-years to build the necessary hospitals and equipment. About a million continuing jobs, including some 100,000 additional doctors, 300,000 nurses, and half a million technicians and other assistants would be needed to keep the hospitals going. Some 600,000 more persons would be needed to produce hospital supplies.

I feel certain that the annual cost of providing complete hospital and health coverage for every person in the nation would not exceed about $25 per person. It might need to vary in particular localities and occupations, according to need and capacity to pay. This cost would cover doctors, nurses, technicians, and assistants—and would include amortization payments on construction facilities

I am heartened by the fact that competent hands are at work on this most important problem, and that the area of disagreement among the experts is fast becoming smaller and smaller. There is, of course, no general disagreement over the need for the construction of hospitals. Some Senators would have the Congress appropriate 2 billion dollars outright to build the necessary hospitals over a ten-year period. Others in private life, like Henry Kaiser and Paul de Kruif, suggest that Congress authorize a Federal Health Housing Authority to guarantee 90 per cent of the construction costs to any group organized sufficiently well to raise 10 per cent of the cost. The Federal authority would pass on the soundness of the plan just as FHA passes on the soundness of plans for housing projects. It would sell bonds either directly or through the Treasury, and the members of the health group would amortize the cost through their annual payments, leaving very little net cost to the Federal government. This approach is in line with traditional American thinking, but it should be noted that if every community does not participate, millions of people would be left unserved. This would be especially true in the South and in many rural areas throughout the country.

It is chiefly in the matter of health insurance where there appear to be differences of opinion. Most people agree that we want prepayment by individuals to cover medical services when the need for them arises—and most people also agree that the use of group facilities should be extended as fast as possible. The only real issue is whether this should be done under a voluntary or compulsory system. But even this issue is not as controversial as it seems. Much of the argument over compulsory as against voluntary insurance, I'm sure, will turn out to have been unnecessary.

There is, of course, a good deal of health insurance of various forms in existence today. Compulsory health insurance, I am sure, does not in the minds of its proponents imply that the voluntary plans in existence today or those that may be organized in the future would have to be liquidated. This is largely a technical problem which the technicians can straighten out—for it is reduced, ultimately, to the simple question of whether the voluntary system can be spread fast enough to give the necessary protection to all. When Congress comes to look into this problem, and as all groups bear in mind Franklin Roosevelt's observation that the health of the people is a paramount responsibility of government, it will find a surprisingly large area of agreement. The major question will be only one of means. And I do not think that differences over *means* will keep the proponents of the two approaches from joining forces to gain the *end* of a healthy nation and a more efficient people.

Whatever approach is used, two things are essential. We must have prompt action. Forty per cent rejection by Selective Service is proof that we have delayed too long. And we must have proper distribution of facilities as well as services. No area, no group, must be left out.

And here again, I want to emphasize that in health—as in housing and education—Federal participation must not lead to Federal control. We must have the maximum amount of community interest, initiative, and responsibility for every ounce of government stimulus or participation.

NEW PIONEERING ON OLD FRONTIERS

Our peace must be as intelligently planned as our war victory. And I can think of no better way to begin than to give the people an honest and realistic preview of just what this country really would look like, and be like, if we applied our knowledge and our experiences to the full development of our resources. We need, for all to see, the grand pattern of the profitable potentials of peace—graphically and factually presented—and prepared by private and public agencies, working and planning together for future profit to the individual groups and to the whole of the nation. Into this pattern of future development would be fitted (1) our existing assets, both public and private; (2) the backlogs of new frontiers for private enterprise; and (3) the nation's own full employment backlog of public projects, including those large-scale developments of natural resources where not only the national interest but also the magnitude of the job call for Federal action if the job is to be done. To finish the grand pattern, there would have to be a co-operative presentation by government and private enterprise showing the new opportunities for private enterprise in the areas of public development

I am sure that if we could only comprehend our potentialities, we would never again have to resort to "leaf-raking" as a way of making work for people whose hands were idle through no fault of their own. And in using the expression "leaf-raking," I am fully aware that not only has it commonly been used by scoffers to cast aspersions upon purely temporary relief work—but that it has also been applied by people of ill-will to the finest and most beneficial of public projects, such as Grand Coulee and the TVA. But I am quite certain my meaning here is unmistakably clear. If we have misused our manpower on "leaf-raking" emergency relief projects in the past, we did so only because of the limitations placed upon Federal authority and because of our failure to prepare long-range plans to hold in readiness for emergency periods.

The development opportunities that must be fitted into this grand pattern are all economically sound—as real as our land, as essential as our rivers, as sturdy as our forests. They make up the nation's own backlog of development and jobs.

River Valley Development. I would estimate, conservatively, that there is between 25 and 30 billion dollars' worth of work in river-valley developments like TVA. This is enough to keep a million men busy for ten years.

Land Conservation. There is from four to five years' work for a million men in long-needed programs of soil conservation, drainage, and irrigation, and in restoration of range land.

Forest Development. There is also from four to five years' work for a million men in forest conservation and in developing recreational facilities in our national and state forests.

Rural Electrification. There are more than 6 million rural homes without electricity—a potential market for more than 5 billion dollars' worth of line construction, installations, electrical appliances and equipment. This would provide close to a million jobs for three years.

The progress we have made in this field, principally due to the stimulus of the Rural Electrification Administration, demonstrates conclusively that one watt of government energy generates many kilowatts of private enterprise. In preparing their own postwar plans, again at the grass roots, for extension of rural service, REA's borrowers alone estimate their expenditures in the first three years after materials and manpower are available, at 579 million dollars—creating indirectly a further demand for 5 billion dollars' worth of goods and services. Finishing the job will provide opportunities for both co-operatives and private power companies. And the record shows that Federal participation in the financing has been on a sound self-liquidating basis—so sound that in many areas, private banks seek to take over the outstanding loans of rural electrification co-operatives. I am indeed proud to have had some part, as Secretary of Agriculture, in such a healthy and practical enterprise.

If we add in the needed airports—both for extension of commercial lines and expansion of private flying—and highway construction, it would be on the conservative side to list upwards of 50 billion dollars in sound public projects in the nation's backlog of full employment in the immediate postwar years. This would be enough to provide a backlog of productive jobs for more than four million persons for five years.

To me, these are exciting opportunities. All too often, we built badly on our old frontiers. We despoiled too much of our national heritage. We squandered resources, ruined land, and wasted forests. Now the old frontiers must be rebuilt. We must pioneer anew. And we have learned how to do it wisely and well—in the manner of free men.

Several years ago I jotted down some ideas on the books that have influenced me. Were I making up the list today, I would include right around the top David Lilienthal's *TVA—Democracy on the March*. In fact, I am inclined to think that it should be on the list of required reading in every high school.

In a review for the *New Republic* I called it one of the

most exciting books that I had read because it describes the new democracy in terms as real as a juicy steak. It makes the TVA live as an example of how a government-inspired project vastly increases the amount of free enterprise and prolongs it far into the future—how the TVA not only enlarges the opportunity for free enterprise, but is a model for decentralized liberty, for true economic democracy, with the people actively and directly participating in the decisions which affect their daily bread.

The TVA epitomizes people planning together in their own community for their own welfare. This planning is not something abstract and remote. It has to do with real things which lie close at hand—soil and fertilizers and soil-erosion control, tree planting, electricity at low rates for home and factory, deep-freeze machines, factory development, barge transportation, pleasure boats, fish in the lakes, and recreation on the shores.

In essence, the TVA is a specific device of administration for rebuilding the old frontiers for thousands of men and women right where they live.

There are areas of activity in which the full benefits can be achieved only through the Federal exploitation of the resources as a whole. This holds true in the development of such a river as the Tennessee, which traverses seven states and which has many possibilities besides those directly exploitable by commercial organizations. This holds true for the development of the Missouri and the Ohio, the great Mississippi itself, and other valleys east of the Alleghenies and west of the Rockies. Achievement of some of the major benefits, such as provision of a navigable channel and control of destructive flood waters, is clearly outside the realm of private enterprise because these activities are not income-producing in the commercial sense. Private enterprise, whatever its size or its virtues, is not equipped to provide such benefits which must pay for themselves in public security and well-being and do not produce immediate monetary profit.

But the function of a regional agency like TVA is much broader than the mere development of the river itself. The full utilization of water resources in the river must be matched by development of the resources of the land, the forests, and the minerals. It is the job of a regional agency, operating with its administrative and technical heads in the field close to the problems at hand, to provide a liaison between the people of the region and the resources upon which they must depend for prosperity. And this type of liaison work is most important to the small private enterprise, whether the family-type farm or the small businessman interested, say, in the exploitation of a relatively obscure mineral resource or in a small agricultural processing plant. Large industries, with concentrations of financial means and research facilities, generally do not need the aid which can be given by a regional agency or by state educational and research institutions with which such a regional Federal agency must normally co-operate. But the record of TVA shows that the small businessman needs this aid, that he is eager for it—and that by using it he profits well.

For the regional agency, by engaging in and encouraging research based on local mineral, forest, and soil resources which it is in a position to explore intimately, constantly creates new opportunities for private enterprise. It provides, moreover, a means of integrating and synthesizing the research efforts of state and private agencies interested in local or regional development. And it gives expert guidance in the utilization of small yet important deposits of minerals, the determination of the exact needs of varying types of soil and the proper use of fertilizers to bring the best results, the development of the right kind of tree crops and the best methods of reforestation—even the improvement of specific types of farm and processing machinery to meet specific needs.

Yes, the TVA is pioneering in new ways to use local ability, incentive, capital, and native capabilities. It is pioneering in perfecting both our political and economic democracy. And in pioneering in the rebuilding of our old frontiers, it is showing the way for the young David Lilienthals of tomorrow—those who must continue to put the bold, brave thoughts of men like George Norris and Franklin Roosevelt into action, for the profit of the many and not just the few, and for the benefit of all.

Yes, the TVA *is* a preview to the resource development of the future.

II

New Horizons in Industry

TECHNOLOGICALLY, the future already is here. Through the veil of wartime secrecy, we have had an occasional hurried glimpse of the marvels of tomorrow. Under the inexorable pressure of war, our laboratories have hastened by many years new discoveries and new perfections in the sciences. We have seen all about us new miracles both in the destruction and the protection of human life. Even the new discoveries for war, when applied to peace, offer vast opportunities for profitable and beneficial pursuits.

We owe it to those who died or were disabled to muster all these scientific and medical advances permanently into the uses of peace. But to use them fully to stimulate the new enterprises without which we can have no full employment, we must have technological freedom as well as political freedom. Manifestly, it is the responsibility of the same government which demanded the full use of all our scientific skill in war—and which financed so much of wartime research and development—also to see to it that the whole nation benefits from these gains in peace. Only if we use our scientific wealth to guarantee a constant flow of new ideas into competitive private enterprise can we maintain an ever-developing frontier in industry.

I do not see upon the immediate technological horizon any new development which will give the same vast stimulus to private enterprise as did the railroads, automobiles, electric power, and the radio. I have recently become an aviation enthusiast, and before this book is off the press, I hope to have my private pilot's license—but I still think the airplane has a long way to go to catch up with the automobile as a source of jobs. However, both commercial and private aviation will have tremendous growth in the postwar years. And even now we may have new processes in other fields which will develop after several years into great new industries now unforeseen.

But wartime improvements upon prewar processes also will have a tremendous aggregate effect upon increasing business. There have been tremendous developments in plastics generally; in silicones (a new family of synthetic resins made from petroleum, brine, and ordinary sand); in the laminated plastics, used in pulleys, panels, and tubes; and, of course, in electronics, with which we can now substitute the "electric eye" for eye skills and human judgment. We may expect great growth of such industries as air-conditioning and refrigeration. And the use of quick-freeze units in our homes may well have radical effects on our whole system of marketing foods.

Research in radio and radar has skipped over decades during the war; and the developments in FM broadcasting and television offer vast new opportunities to the postwar radio industry. New wonders in chemicals and synthetics touch thousands of articles in daily use—medical products, rubber products, gasoline and oils, paints, dyestuffs, and plastics. And the superautomobiles of the future—which our present engineering knowledge, light metals, super fuels, and wartime advances in engine design make possible—will require an abundance of superhighways like the great Pennsylvania Pike.

Our magnesium production increased 35 times between 1939 and 1943. Millions of dollars were invested by our government in wartime magnesium plants. And the men who develop new peacetime uses for magnesium will save several large communities built around these great plants.

Inventive genius and technological know-how are among our most valuable national assets. National industrial growth and national security demand that we constantly broaden our scientific horizons. However, our smug complacency about our scientific leadership has been shaken considerably in recent years—first, by the shocking revelations of the world-wide influence of German cartels; and second, by Germany's own amazing development and rapid application of new and improved war weapons. As a result, I am sure we now realize that in the world of tomorrow we shall have to be constantly alert if we are to hold our own in science and technology.

But free enterprise will be shackled and restrained if research is dominated by a small number of large corporations and cartels. This control has already barred small businessmen from many of our industrial developments. Certainly, the application of modern science should not be the exclusive domain of great corporations and cartels which can, if they desire, restrict and suppress new inventions and scientific information to suit their private interests instead of the public interest.

Our technological civilization often requires, in the public 'nterest, the pooling of patents and know-how by large corporations to build a better product for mass distribution. But unless the little man also has access to the bounties of technology, free enterprise will suffer to the detriment of the full employment of labor and our resources.

Small business cannot support the large and costly laboratories which are necessary for modern industrial research. Most of our advanced research is concentrated today in about 100 companies; and this concentration inevitably results in the restricted use of scientific information and know-how. Thousands of small businesses are thus kept from utilizing the discoveries of science. To fill this need, I believe the Federal government should make research facilities available to them.

The field of agriculture offers a lesson for industrial research. For more than two generations the government has taken an active part in conducting, sponsoring, and co-ordinating research. In fact, by far the greater part of all research done in agriculture has been initiated or aided by the government. I do not wish to detract from the credit which is quite properly being given to the farmers, food handlers, farm machinery manufacturers, processors, and distributors for the amazing job which is being done in feeding and clothing a large part of the world. I believe that they should receive all the credit which we have been giving them—and more. But I don't believe anyone will seriously dispute with me the statement that their ability to achieve these notable results is due largely to the vast number of improvements in crop production, handling, and processing which the years have brought. And here, the Department of Agriculture, the various state experiment stations financed jointly by the Federal government and the states, and the four great regional agricultural laboratories furnish abundant and conclusive proof of the benefits of government research.

I know full well that there are immense fields of necessary research which cannot and should not be the sole concern of private companies whose primary aim and responsibility is to further the interest of their stockholders. These companies, particularly the industrial giants, have done and are doing a marvelous job of industrial research. But one needs to focus attention not upon the advance which has been made, but rather upon that which might have been made and was not made—and upon what should be made and may not be made. In not a few instances, the blame for lack of advance rests squarely on the shoulders of private interests whose selfishness has blocked advance. But in a far-larger number of situations, the failure to move forward is not the fault of any single company or of any group. Rather, I think it is due to the lack of an overall agency which is so constituted as to take the long view and so equipped as to do something about it. Public-supported research has done exactly that in the field of agriculture.

THE FEDERAL GOVERNMENT AND TECHNOLOGY

Increasingly, technology has become a concern of statecraft. The abrupt impact of science often produces maladjustments in our own economy and in the economic life of other countries. New inventions often result in immediate hardship to some group. The locomotive put the canals and canalmen out of business and stopped much of the navigation on our Western rivers. The threshing crews were ousted by the combine. And it is estimated that the mechanical cotton-picker after the war may take a livelihood, meager as it is, away from some 2 million cotton-pickers in the South.

Yet few would argue against great new inventions and processes because they bring temporary hardship to certain groups. In the main they have, in net balance, raised living standards, created new industries, and increased the nation's wealth and overall productivity. They pose what might be called a *permanent problem of reconversion*—the problem of how to get the greatest advance from new inventions with the least cost in terms of industrial and labor displacement. Government must be competently organized to meet such situations, and to work out fair and just solutions. But to do this, government requires sufficient technical resources and information to formulate technological policies and to put them into action whenever the general welfare demands. From our experiences in peace and war, I would suggest the following program:

1. There should be established a central technical authority of the Federal government. This authority should co-ordinate the increasing activities of the government in scientific fields. It should not dictate the methods to be carried out by existing Federal scientific bureaus, but should serve as a clearing house for these organizations.

2. Every business and institution should have full access

to all inventions and research findings which have been developed at government expense. The Congress has provided large sums of money, which are being poured into Federal, university, and industrial laboratories. It is the intention of the Congress that this money be spent for the benefit of the general public, not for the exclusive benefit of a few corporations. Likewise, the enemy patents seized by the Alien Property Custodian should become the property of the Federal government and be made available to all businesses.

3. Federal support should be continued in the postwar period. There are many fields of research which are not fully covered by existing private laboratories; Federal support should be made available in these fields. I believe that Federal funds should support especially (a) fundamental science, the mother of applied science, upon which the welfare and prosperity of the nation rests; (b) research and development wherever it affects national interest, such as in national defense, public health, public housing, and the balanced regional development of the entire nation. The Federal government should see to it that there is no concentration of benefits of this research in specific institutions or areas.

4. Technical information for small business should be made available by the Federal government through technical information offices in each state. Moreover, the state centers should initiate research projects of special importance to their area.

I see absolutely no conflict between this proposed program and existing private research. Instead, I can see only mutual stimulation—that is, if we assume that competitive free enterprise means the balanced growth of all industries, big and small, and that the common goal is not scarcity, but abundance.

THE SOUTH—A SUMMATION OF
NEW FRONTIERS

In an early chapter—pointing out what full employment means to the businessman in the way of opportunities for expanded markets for low-priced, mass-produced, and mass-distributed consumer goods—I stressed the importance of rediscovering our economic frontiers at home, with a special reference to the South. Later, I emphasized what the elimination of wage differentials would mean, not just in new opportunities for the South, but for the whole of the nation. In this chapter, I have given a partial listing of these new frontiers of opportunities in our own land. And here again, I point to the South as a summation, in itself, of these opportunities.

The South long has been in need of shifting from too great a dependence on cotton and tobacco to diversified farming and to nonfarming industries. The TVA has helped materially—and manufacturing has grown somewhat faster in the South than in the rest of the country in recent decades. But this industrialization process has only begun.

What the South needs is a long-range reconversion program which would put farming on a more efficient and more profitable basis, thereby stimulating the growth of nonagricultural industries, and thus create an opportunity for more farm people in industry. The South would then get a larger proportion of the nation's jobs.

This reconversion and industrialization program would require an increase of 5 million in nonfarm employment in the South—that is, from 8 million in 1940 to 13 million by the middle fifties. The bulk of the increase would be in the manufacturing industries, in trade and service occupations. The gap between per capita earnings in the South and those in the North always has been deplorably wide. But with an industrial reconversion program, both farm and nonfarm income and purchasing power in the South would be at least doubled and would thus approach the average per capita income for the rest of the country.

For many years, as I pointed out in an earlier chapter, the South and the West were the victims of a vicious system of freight-rate discriminations—always a factor for discouraging industrial progress. By its recent decision equalizing freight rates, the Supreme Court has served well the cause of industrial progress in the South, as in the West.

To put the Southern reconversion program into effect calls for widely diversified planning. And some idea of the scope of the job can be seen in a program recently set forth by the Department of Agriculture as essential to the development of the South's potentialities. To some the recommendations may seem to be too commonplace and too elementary for discussion. But any Chamber of Commerce executive in any city or town will know how real and basic are the following points:

1. Every community must become a planning center—to survey what the community can consume in industrial and

farm products, and to find ways to expand local industries or establish new ones.

2. In judging what industrial opportunities are possible in the various localities, specific research and technical information must be had—dealing with the available resources, with the requirements for labor and capital, with production costs, and transportation facilities. The communities must be able to look to state, regional, or Federal agencies to fill their need.

3. With the diversified farm production that goes along with industrialization, and with a growing industrial population, additional and new food-marketing and -processing facilities must be planned in advance.

4. Job-placement and -training services must be provided for farm people who will want to take up industrial work in their own communities or elsewhere.

5. Where local private capital is not available, Federal aid must be made available for industrial development. This could be provided by the RFC, the Federal Reserve Banks, or the Smaller War Plants Corporation, if it is retained in some form for peacetime development.

6. Plans must be made for the expansion of public utilities, including railroads, streetcar and bus service, production and distribution of electric power, telephone and telegraph lines; and for the expansion of other public facilities, such as highway, sewer and water systems, schools and hospitals, and post offices. Advance planning of these facilities, and legislative provision for their construction prior to their need, would give to every community a clear idea of its own backlog of jobs.

Finally, industrialization in the South, to stand up against the competition of other areas, will need both increased productivity and greater consumption on the part of both the white and Negro working population. This cannot be had without raising the general level of health and education.

I have already specifically mentioned several notable instances of community and state planning in the South. Actually, similar progress is being made in many other communities. For as I have repeatedly noted, community planning and stimulation of new enterprise—in short, community responsibility—must be the basis of action in our democratic life.

To bring 5 million more workers into Southern industry—to more than double the per capita income of the Southern farm and industrial population—to raise the level of health and living standards of a third of our total population—and to bring these results about through billions of dollars of private investment, with Federal stimulation where needed—this, indeed, is an exciting peacetime task. If the South can meet this challenge, it will be helping immeasurably to guarantee continued full employment for all the nation.

III

New Frontiers Abroad

THE INDUSTRIAL REVOLUTION as yet has brought very few benefits, if any, to the great bulk of the 2 billion people in the world.

Three quarters of the world's peoples—in most of Asia and Africa, and in much of Central and South America, and even some of southern Europe—still make little use of machinery in city industry or on farms. They still use most of their population on the land, producing a bare minimum of food and clothing by primitive means.

Modern science and modern tools and equipment can increase the productivity and raise the wages and standards of living of men of all races—white and yellow, brown and black—of all languages, and of all countries, in the same way as it has raised that of northern and western Europe and North America in the past century and a half—and that of Soviet Russia in the past quarter century. This process of industrial and agricultural development over the world will open up an unlimited new frontier of opportunities for the investment of American funds and the work of American hands and brains. Our stake in helping these nations to develop their opportunities can be counted as part of our backlog for many years to come.

Our first big postwar job abroad, of course, is to help restore some sort of order in the devastated areas, and get farm and factory production running again. Repairing the war devastation, plus the initial steps toward industrialization in backward countries, will require from 55 to 65 billion dollars' worth of plant and equipment in the few years immediately after the war. Approximately half of this could easily come from the United States if suitable arrangements for its financing were worked out. Moreover, relief needs for food and clothing will mean a continued large demand. And this immediate postwar demand overseas—although much less than our enormous wartime shipments—will help us materially in the process of shifting from an economy sending half its products to war areas abroad back to an economy devoting nine tenths of its products to the consumption of its own people.

But many thorny questions must be settled before the restoration job abroad can get fully under way. What industries will postwar Germany be permitted to operate? And Japan? How self-sufficient will eastern Europe and the Soviet Union be—and how much interchange will they have with the rest of the world? Who will finance and operate the restored railways, air lines, and communications of central and western Europe—a United Nations authority, or the occupation authorities? These are but typical of the many problems—in Europe and in the Far East—whose answers depend in part on political decisions— but they must be faced openly and answered promptly, so that the way can be cleared for financial, industrial, and agricultural operations based on definite understandings.

In these devastated areas, both of our liberated allies and of the enemy, reconstruction cannot be separated from the long-range problems of industrialization and development. In considering these problems, it must be borne in mind that other regions of the world are also eager to undertake long-range expansion programs. Their demands and needs must be considered along with the demand and need of reconstruction. In fact, the program of industrial and agricultural development today must be guided by a strong sense of the broad shape of things to come everywhere in the future world—for men must have an ideal and a dream before they can build effectively. Let us see, then, some of the broad outlines of development opportunities—and job opportunities—elsewhere in the world in the first decade or two of peace.

Latin America offers enormous possibilities for future development. In part, it is a region of thinly settled tropical forests or high semiarid mountain plateaus—much of which man has not yet learned to use effectively. In part, it is highly productive and thickly populated tropical coasts or islands. And in part, it is like our own rich Mississippi Valley. Its wealth of metals and minerals is vast and only partly explored. In South America vast river systems carry most of the commerce in the interior. And with their tributaries flowing from high mountains, these systems offer great opportunities for hydroelectric developments. Despite these advantages, the region as a whole is only partially developed, and returns only a scanty existence to most of the people. The rich resources have been developed mainly for export, often by foreign-owned companies, and most of the region has been kept in a colonial stage of development. Industries for home consumption have been extensively developed in Argentina, Mexico, and Brazil, and to a lesser extent in Colombia, Cuba, and Chile; while an eager interest in industrial development exists in all the rest of the Latin American countries. But even in the countries of most development, only the surface has been scratched.

The United States government has stimulated some progress through loans and grants for scientific research and development projects, especially for war-connected lines such as rubber, vegetable oils, metals, and minerals. But the region as a whole is in need of modern science and technology as applied to agriculture and industry; it is in need of curative and preventive sanitation and health measures for men, beasts, and crops; and it is in particular need of expanded facilities for education. On the physical side, transportation and communication facilities, water and sewerage for many of its cities, and other public services for modern life, are needed to open the way for future expansion.

In the past, the United States has had a larger foreign trade with the 12 million people of Canada than with all 140 million people of Latin America. Surely, then, here is an abundance of new frontiers of opportunity for our factories and for our industrial and scientific know-how—a profitable opportunity for future development, not on the colonial basis of the selfish and ruinous exploitation so common to the days of dollar diplomacy, but on the basis of mutual respect and of building a lasting and ever-expanding market for the products of free enterprise.

Southern and southeast Asia embraces nearly half of the world's population—and it also offers almost half of the development opportunities. From Iran through India, Burma, French Indo-China, and on to the Philippines— here is an area where the population is enormous, consumption is on a subsistence basis, and standards of life are generally exceedingly low. Population pressure is extremely severe. India alone, in the last ten years, added to its population the equivalent of the entire population of the British Isles. Modern science or technology is virtually unknown, except in a few industrial centers. Popular education is generally absent or inadequate. Interest in health and sanitation is just beginning. But still, native thought and aspirations—as expressed, for example, in the industrial proposals of the Bombay Group in India—look to a rapid development in the future. For these peoples, too, have witnessed or experienced or suffered from the might of industrial civilizations in global war. And like others elsewhere in the world, they contemplate the benefits of an industrial civilization in peace. They have a long way to go—but they want to get going.

One of the real tests of the Allied victors will be the extent to which they encourage and aid the future development of this great region. With adequate agricultural and industrial development, the vast population of this region can become one of the greatest producing and consuming markets in the world.

But the biggest frontier of future development will be found with the new dawn in the northern Pacific and eastern Asia.

After V-J Day—after our boys have landed back on home shores at Seattle or Portland, San Francisco or Los Angeles —then we shall think more and more of our West as the link with the East of Asia. Those who believe that East is East and West is West and never the twain shall meet are wrong. The East of Asia, both Chinese and Russian, is on the march in a way which is easy for any American to understand who sees these great areas at first hand for himself. The rapid agricultural and industrial development of these peoples means so very much to the peace and prosperity of the entire postwar world.

Our Northwest was long held back by unfair freight rates and by failure to develop the power of its mighty rivers. But thanks to men like Roosevelt and Norris, McNary and Bone, the Northwest during the past ten years has rapidly expanded. This expansion must continue to the limit of its agricultural, industrial, and commercial potentialities. This includes Alaska, which has not yet begun to measure up to its possibilities. But this growth must be not merely in national terms, but also in terms of Asia. Vigorous two-way trade with Soviet Asia and China will greatly increase the population and prosperity of our Northwest and the whole of our people.

All of this I knew in a theoretical way before going to Asia in 1944. After having seen something of the industry and agriculture of East Asia, I am more than ever convinced that we are entering upon what might be called the Era of the Pacific. One characteristic of the Pacific Era will be the building of great airports in parts of the world now very thinly inhabited. The extent to which the Russians have already developed runways and servicing for airplanes in East Asia amazed me. We landed at perhaps a dozen airports in Soviet Asia, the names of which not one in a thousand Americans has ever heard. It is quite possible that for a decade or two after this war the air route to Asia via Fairbanks, Alaska, may not be much of a money-maker. But it is also certain that our national future and our national interest require that we, in co-operation with Russia and the Chinese, keep the route open.

Soviet Asia during the past fifteen years has more than doubled in population. It is quite possible that the next fifty years will see a further increase of more than 30 million people. I am convinced that in the southern part of the Amur River region, particularly, there will be a great increase in population and industrial activity. For Russia, as a result of her experience with this war, will certainly shift much of her industry east of the Urals.

China is totally different from Soviet Asia. While the Chinese are eager to enter the machine age, they have not yet been able to manufacture more than a small fraction of their needs. This situation should not long continue. China, with her 450 million people and her great resources, should sooner or later produce a large portion of her requirements in the way of heavy and light industrial goods and also consumer goods. To modernize her industry and train her people China needs help. We have thousands of technical men and businessmen in the United States who are able to furnish that help. But the businessmen want and need to be sure of one thing. They want to be certain, before they lay the foundations and make the necessary outlays, that there is no foreseeable likelihood of continued conflict within China or conflict between China and the USSR.

Postwar stability in China is dependent upon economic reconstruction—agricultural as well as industrial—and reconstruction in China is dependent upon trade and finance. This reconstruction, moreover, depends upon imports from abroad. It will require technical and material assistance from us, given on a businesslike basis, in the development of agricultural and industrial facilities and technology, in scientific research, and in sanitation and public health.

The American businessman of tomorrow must have a broad world outlook. Given this, I have faith that American economic leadership can confer on the Pacific region a great material benefit and on the world a great blessing. This limitless new frontier holds countless resources of minerals and manpower to be developed by democratic, peaceful, and co-operative methods—not by the methods of "dollar diplomacy" exploitation, but by the method of creating higher living standards for hundreds of millions of people. And as we help other peoples to build their own better life—with a material benefit to us in the bargain—we can also help them to profit from our own mistakes.

Our Tennessee Valley Authority has stirred the imagination of all the world. The peoples of underdeveloped areas everywhere have heard how we transformed one of our most backward regions into one of the most developed. All over the world today, men with vision are looking at their great rivers, at the appalling devastation their floods produce, at the unchecked erosion and loss of soil in their drainage basins—they want to know whether their own river systems offer similar opportunities for public action to open up new frontiers of co-ordinated industrial and agricultural development. The Balkans and the Danube; India's great Ganges basin; the vast river systems of South America; China's Yellow River, "the Sorrow of China," with its recurrent floods and yellow silt-laden waters; the Yangtze, with enormous power possibilities; and Palestine's Jordan and the vast arid plains which in ancient times were watered by the Tigris and the Euphrates—the challenge of these new frontiers should stimulate us for many years to come.

For many years I have had a deep interest in these new frontiers abroad. When I was Secretary of Agriculture, it was my good fortune to have had something to do with sending Walter C. Lowdermilk, one of the world's ablest soil-conservation experts, to the Near East to survey the land and river potentialities of that area. Later, Dr. Lowdermilk told the world of the extensive development opportunities he found there, in his exciting book, *Palestine —Land of Promise.*

Faced with these possibilities for manifold industrial development abroad, this country must do some hard thinking, and make some courageous decisions if it is to avoid the mistakes of the last twenty-five years. The wartime accumulated demand abroad will help make markets for American goods for a time, just as they did after the last war. Part of our exports can be paid for at first by the large dollar reserves many countries have built up during the war, when we were buying heavily from them for war purposes and sending little to them in return. This is particularly true of Latin American countries. But if we do not become bigger buyers of the goods of other countries than we were before the war—and if high tariff barriers continue to block certain imports from many countries—the business based on large exports will again prove as ephemeral as it was in the twenties, and the resulting economic collapse will be more severe than that of the early thirties.

To avert such disaster, we must learn to regard imports as being just as important to us as exports. We must think of foreign trade as a two-way street. As foreign countries regain or establish their productive power, we must be as zealous in looking for opportunities to buy goods and services from them as we are in trying to sell things to them. By having cut them off from foreign sources of much of their normal imports, even though briefly, this war has made many Americans realize for the first time how much of their usual comfortable living depended on products imported from abroad. Shortages of tin, rubber, petroleum, silk, oils and fats, sugar, coffee, tea, spices, bananas, flax, pineapples, dates, nuts, cocoa, and many other imported products have made life harder and less enjoyable, forcing housewives to alter radically many of their accustomed menus. As these and other foreign goods again become available, we must learn to realize that the real prosperity of nations depends not on what we all sell, but upon what we all consume. Our businessmen, in their travels abroad, should seek not merely new markets for our own goods; they should also seek out and bring back for the greater richness of American life all the varied goods and specialty products of the craftsmen of other countries. On top of that, foreign travel everywhere can provide other useful means of sharing in what other nations can produce for our use and enjoyment—in recreation, rest, and culture as well as in material things.

In all these ways, our own businessmen and the businessmen of foreign nations, exploring and pioneering in new fields of useful international exchange, can find new ways by which billions of American dollars can usefully be spent abroad, so that foreigners in turn can send those dollars back to us to pay for the autos and machinery and apples and cotton that they need year after year—and to pay the charges on their loans from us. To escape a repetition of the disasters of the twenties and thirties, we must build up the national policies and the business arrangements that will make foreign trade a permanent two-way street—not a temporary detour to a precipice.

For the immediate postwar period, these frontiers abroad, together with high levels of activity here at home, should support an international trade far above previous peacetime levels. If we have full employment at good wages in this country—together with the assurance of continued peace, the continuation of a sensible trade-agreements program and stability in foreign exchange—our people should bring in at least 7 billion dollars' worth of goods and services annually from abroad, and spend from 1 to 2 billions abroad on foreign travel and other services. Foreign countries would draw on their accumulated dollar balances, say

1 billion a year, and we would make new foreign loans of from 2 to 4 billions a year. During the peak of the initial postwar industrialization the figures might be larger than this and our exports for a time might reach much larger proportions.

As we approach the end of this period, we shall face the problem of whether we prefer to expand still further our purchases of foreign goods and services, or to contract our volume of exports. In either case, corresponding adjustments will be needed in our economy at home, if we are to make the shifts necessary to continue full employment.

INTERNATIONAL MEASURES TO AID POSTWAR EXPANSION

The United Nations now recognize that one reason the last peace did not endure was because it did not deal adequately with economic problems. They are now determined that the new peace will be broad and comprehensive enough to establish the necessary economic foundations for a peaceful world. To this end, they arranged at San Francisco for world security and world order. But long before San Francisco, under Franklin Roosevelt's brilliant and farsighted leadership, the United Nations had been conferring together on the economic measures necessary for postwar world co-operation.

At Hot Springs, in 1943, the Food and Agriculture Conference devised means by which the nations might co-operate to insure their peoples better foods and their farmers more prosperity. The new Food and Agriculture Organization of the United Nations will be the focal point through which the agricultural departments, the public-health departments, farm organizations, and consumers' groups of all the nations can work together on these problems—and help the undeveloped nations apply modern science and technology to crops, livestock, forests, fisheries, and food.

The Bretton Woods Monetary and Financial Conference, in 1944, devised plans for two international organizations, a Stabilization Fund and an Investment Bank. The Fund will seek to prevent the kind of chaos in international exchange rates which prevailed after the last war; to outlaw exchange control as an instrument of economic warfare—and through its pooled assets, to lend a helping hand to any nation that needs to be helped over temporary difficulties in meeting its foreign exchange requirements, and to help it work out more lasting economic readjustments if its foreign balances seem to be in chronic distress. The Bank, on the other hand, is a central source of investment funds both for rebuilding industries shattered by the war and for initiating new industrial developments in undeveloped countries. Its loans will come from its public capital, or from private underwriters with the Bank guaranteeing them against loss. In either case, the Bank will make loans only if no private sources are available at reasonable rates. By taking the most risky loans, the Bank will encourage private investors to put their funds into other less risky enterprises in the same areas—just as our publicly supported land-grant railroads after the Civil War encouraged vast private investments in opening up the Midwest and West. Again, an ounce of pooled governmental activity, on a world basis, would create a pound and more of private activity in an undeveloped area.

The Bank loans will differ from our foreign lending of the twenties in three respects: (1) while we again put up much of the capital, all nations will share in the risk of loss, pro rata to their wealth; (2) loans will be made at reasonable interest rates with long-time amortization periods instead of at the excessive interest rates and high underwriters' fees which made it impossible for borrowers to pay out on much of our foreign loans of the twenties; and (3) loans will be made only on sound productive projects, approved by a committee of the world's best experts, whereas, last time, many of them went for a variety of unproductive purposes. By these arrangements, the Bank will finance directly part of the development of the new foreign frontiers, and will stimulate a great deal of related private investment, while at the same time protecting the interest of the investing nations.

Early in the first Roosevelt administration, we became a member of the International Labour Organization, which works for world industrial betterment on the labor front. The ILO is especially important as a force to see to it that as rapidly as any country raises the levels of efficiency and production of its workers, it reflects those gains in higher wages and better conditions of work for its own workers. This is most important. For in the past, nations such as Japan could improve their production processes, keep their workers at low wages and poor standards, under sell other countries in world markets, and use the money to accumulate steel, iron, rubber, and oil for militaristic adventures. It is the job of the ILO to keep us all alert so that this kind of exploitation cannot happen again.

The United Nations have made great progress in thinking through how to clear the way for more foreign trade after the war, instead of the steadily contracting foreign trade of before the war. Ideas already discussed revolve around three lines of work. First, measures to reduce trade barriers, including a speeding up of our own trade-agreements program, and measures to insure that regulation of foreign exchange and commerce will not be used as a means to throttle commerce. Second, measures to end private and irresponsible monopoly in international trade by which great corporations, operating through international cartels, have hitherto held down industrial developments in many countries, and restricted international development and trade in the interest of the few. Third, international regulation of governmental commodity agreements through a central office which will work for the benefit of consumers as well as producers on a world-wide basis. I would also expect that another specialized international organization—an international trade unit—will be established to encourage and aid expanding world commerce, and to develop and recommend whatever measures are needed. Through such an organization, the departments of commerce or boards of trade of every government, the associations of exporters and importers, and other public and private groups interested in foreign trade can maintain contact with one another in the interests of a continually expanding and mutually beneficial international commerce among all nations.

Beyond these specific economic organizations, the nations will work together on many social and cultural problems—education, health, medicine, and the interchange of arts and sciences. Already there have been specific United Nations discussions on education looking toward a permanent international organization. And the numerous Inter-American meetings on widely varying subjects, such as health, physical education, population, and land tenure, foreshadow new fields of United Nations activity. In addition, many specific problems—oil, air services, European inland transportation, maritime shipping rates, wheat, cotton—have been explored in special conferences. Finally, to prevent confusion and duplication among these varied specialized international organizations, the Social and Economic Council of the general United Nations organization will be a general co-ordinator, protecting the interests of all.

Thus I feel certain that American business can look upon new opportunities abroad with new confidence. But foreign trade must not become a contest for supremacy among nations. Economic warfare is as destructive of prosperity as military warfare. Modern science points the way to growth and improvement for all; the nations must work with, not against, those underlying trends. The world is on the move to a better life. In that march forward, this nation must accept a great share in the responsibility for achievement. And doing this, it will share in the rewards.

PART FIVE

The Budget for Abundance

I

The Nation's Budget for Full Employment

FROM THE foregoing we know something of our responsibilities, and we know something of what I have called the grand pattern of our potential peacetime development —an outline of the new frontiers of our development, private and public, at home and abroad. The problem before us becomes one of finding the proper means of making the necessary adjustments in our democratic processes—(1) so that we can continue to function as a free people to the best of our capacities to produce and consume, and (2) so that we can best utilize our grand pattern to provide us with full employment.

Let us suppose that the people, through their representatives in the Congress, agree that the responsibility for providing full employment must be made the responsibility of the Federal government—with due regard for, and relying upon support from, the strength of community desire for action. And let us suppose that the Congress is ready to pass the necessary legislation. What, then, should that legislation provide?

There will be 60 million jobs when there is a market for all the products that 60 million people at work can turn out. With a work week of 40 hours, and with present levels of prices, this would mean a national production of around 200 billion dollars' worth of goods and services a year. How can we, as a nation, maintain this 200-billion-dollar market? What can we have our government do to assure this market for us, within the framework of our democratic system?

There are several ways by which the Federal government could pretty well assure and maintain this necessary 200-billion-dollar market. One extreme way would be to resort to the so-called "Planned Economy" of the regimented state—whereby the Federal government would assign people to jobs, fix wages and prices, and control practically every other jot and tittle of our national life. But this would not be an American way.

Another extreme method would be to issue per capita amounts of money to everyone, irrespective of whether a person has a job or not—or whether he wants to work or not. This was actually proposed by the Social Credit fringe, which believed that the quickest way to guarantee purchasing power would be to distribute greenbacks to every citizen. The cost, according to the advocates, wouldn't matter—because the government could always print more greenbacks. But this, too, would not be our way.

A third way would be for the government to make an outright commitment, irrespective of the cost, to give work to everyone who wants a job but cannot find one—and who applies at a public employment office for a public job. The government could do this—and it could put the people to work on useful public projects. But our free-enterprise system would not thrive for long in such an unhealthful climate of concern over the cost in taxes and the competition of government. Then, too, such an employment policy inevitably would lead us to state regimentation.

We must find the proper balance between liberty and control, between stimulating full employment and keeping free enterprise free. I believe the national budget—representative of all segments of our national life—provides the answer.

I believe the people should direct the government to prepare a national budget—a budget covering not merely the expenditures and receipts of the Federal government, but also covering everything that would be bought and consumed each year by all segments of the nation. This would cover the total of all our production; the total purchases of goods and services by consumers, the purchases of goods and services by business (for replacement and expansion), and the purchases of goods and services by the Federal and state and local governments. To provide for prompt action for situations where this national budget showed that the national market was not going to be big enough to keep people fully employed, the government should be directed to prepare a program that would promote the maximum of private expenditure and the minimum of government expenditure to produce the necessary total national production. For situations where the national budget showed too much was going to be spent and there was danger of inflation, the government should be directed to take steps to hold down expenditures in line with potentially available supplies of goods and services.

WHAT THE NATION'S BUDGET MEANS

We all know what a personal budget looks like—income on one side, expenses listed on the other, and savings left over—if we are lucky enough to have any. Businessmen are familiar with a budget for a business concern—only they call it a tentative forecast of a profit-and-loss statement—receipts on one side, expenses on the other, and any excess or deficit as profit or loss. The traditional state or Federal budget also shows receipts listed on one side, expenditures on the other, and resulting surplus or deficit. Any one of these budgets—personal, business, or government—may be an actual record covering a time already past, or may be an estimate or forecast for the year ahead. The purely Federal budget that the President now sends to the Congress each January is both a record and a forecast, covering Federal receipts and expenditures for the past and current year, estimated receipts for the fiscal year ahead, and proposed expenditures to be voted by Congress for that year.

When Franklin Roosevelt sent his last budget to Congress, he added a budget for the entire nation. This nation's budget brought together in a single summary statement the budgets of all the families, all the businesses, and all the government units of the nation. He did not attempt to forecast this budget for a year ahead: he merely presented a historical budget which showed what had happened to the nation's spending thus far in the war, as contrasted with prewar years. I take my hat off to Franklin Roosevelt and Budget Director Harold Smith for presenting this concise summary of the greatest business in the world— the income and expenditures of the American people.

The nation's budget is made up of four parts—(1) what consumers receive and spend; (2) what businesses take in and spend; (3) what local and state governments receive and spend; and (4) what the Federal government receives and spends.

PARTS OF THE NATION'S BUDGET

1. The Consumers' Budget. For 1939, for example, the budgets of consumers (including unincorporated businesses) added up as follows (in billions of dollars):

	Receipts	Disbursements
CONSUMERS' BUDGET:		
Net income received	70.8	
Less taxes, etc.	3.5	
Income available for expenditures	67.3	
Spent for goods and services		61.7
Saved (loaned to others)		5.6
Totals	67.3	67.3

Thus, over and above what they spent for their own uses, the consumers set aside as a whole, 5.6 billions in savings.

2. The Business Budget. The consolidated budget for all business enterprise the same year was:

BUSINESS BUDGET:	Receipts	Disbursements
Net income earned	5.5	
Plus reserves for depreciation, etc.	7.7	
	13.2	
Less taxes, etc., paid	1.1	
Dividends paid	3.8	
Income available for expenditures	8.3	
Spent for plant equipment, inventories, etc.		10.9
Borrowed from others	2.6	
Totals	10.9	10.9

Business not only invested all its own spare funds, but also borrowed 2.6 billions from others and spent that, too.

3. Local and State Governments. The consolidated 1939 budget for all state and local governments was:

LOCAL AND STATE GOVERNMENT BUDGET:	Received	Spent
Receipts from taxes, etc.	8.9	
Spent for all purposes		9.1
Borrowed from others	0.2	
Total	9.1	9.1

Tax receipts almost covered local and state government expenditures, and 0.2 billions were borrowed to balance the spendings.

4. *Federal Government.* The Federal budget for the same year was:

FEDERAL GOVERNMENT BUDGET:	Received	Spent
Receipts from taxes, etc.	6.5	
Spent for all purposes		9.3
Borrowed from others	2.8	
Total	9.3	9.3

How Savings Were Used. These separate parts show how net savings were put to work. Bring them together and they show:

Net savings of consumers	5.6	
Net borrowings of business		2.6
Net borrowings of state and local governments		0.2
Net borrowings of Federal government		2.8
	5.6	5.6

Putting these summaries together, and setting aside saving and lending in a separate column, these sectors of the economy can be summarized in a national budget as shown in Table I, which follows:

TABLE I. THE NATIONAL BUDGET
FOR 1939
(billions)

	Receipts	Expendi- tures	Borrow- ing (−) or Lend- ing (+)
CONSUMERS:			
Income after taxes	$ 67.3		
Goods and services bought		$ 61.7	
Savings			$ + 5.6
BUSINESS:			
Undistributed profits and reserves	$ 8.3		
Expenditures on capital formation		$ 10.9	
Borrowings			$ − 2.6
LOCAL AND STATE GOVERN- MENTS:			
Receipts	$ 8.9		
Expenditures		$ 9.1	
Borrowings			$ − 0.2
FEDERAL GOVERNMENT:			
Receipts	$ 6.5		
Expenditures		$ 9.3	
Borrowings			$ − 2.8
Less duplications [1]	$ − 2.4	$ − 2.4	
Total: Gross National Product			
Receipts	$ 88.6		
Expenditures		$ 88.6	

[1] Mainly government expenditures that add directly to personal incomes.

This table shows that the nation's budget balanced out at 88.6 billion dollars in 1939. But let us not be fooled by this bookkeeping balance. The total of incomes of these four sectors necessarily equals the total of their expenditures. Unfortunately, the nation's budget was balanced at too low a level. Both spending and producing were too small to give full employment. More than 7 millions were still unemployed in that year.

PREPARING THE NATION'S BUDGET

The Federal government, of course, has to make its estimates of Federal operation a year or more in advance. The national budget, however, will need to be reappraised at short intervals, perhaps every quarter, to allow for changing conditions.

At first glance it might seem to be impossible to prepare such a budget, for no one is wise enough to say ahead of time exactly how each one of our 60 million jobholders and business units, or their families, will use their money. Nor, in a democracy, can government tell them how to spend their money. But we do know that insurance companies can safely sell us insurance to protect us against fire or accident or death—even though no company can tell which particular house will burn, or which particular man will die in a natural death, next month or next year. The insurance company, in the actuarial tables, depends on the laws of large numbers. In the same way, without saying which individual will buy what car, or which one will prefer to buy a house, business and government statisticians, pooling their resources, can estimate pretty closely from past experience and current trends how a large group of consumers will react to more income or less income, how much of their income farmers will spend for machinery, and how much business will use for new investment. In addition, direct reports would be obtained from business concerns and from farmers on their programs for investment and expenditure in factories and machinery.

As an example of information that is going to be available to business and government, already manufacturers have reported to the Department of Commerce that during the first twelve months after V-E Day their planned expenditures for plant and equipment would amount to 4.5 billion dollars. This amount is substantially greater than that of 1939 or 1929. The actual expenditures will, of course, depend on the material and labor supply.

Making up such a budget, then, would include keeping track of how much money consumers are likely to have in the form of wages, savings, and dividends, and just how much of that purchasing power the consumers are likely to spend for goods and services. It would also be necessary to estimate how much money business will have during the year as a result of profits and borrowing, and how many jobs business will create as a result of investing that money in buildings, machines, and tools.

If after considering all possible ways in which action by government can stimulate both consumers and businessmen to spend more, and the conclusion is reached that there is serious unemployment ahead—then government must consider how much money it must spend to provide useful jobs so as to encourage business to take over a larger proportion of the burden of supplying jobs as rapidly as possible.

The President, in submitting the national full-employment budget to Congress each January, would give his appraisal of current job-creating expenditures by business and consumers. If it seems likely that they will not spend enough to furnish full employment, then it would be the duty of the President to suggest two specific types of incentives. One type involves no government spending, but would embrace such nonspending devices as tax and credit incentives to stimulate both consumers and businessmen to spend more and therefore to create more jobs. The other type of incentive would include the use of government funds, either as grants-in-aid to states or localities for public works, or for actual investment directly by the Federal government in development of our resources. And just as I have pointed out previously that our programs of public works must be approved by the engineers and plans prepared well in advance of their need —so as to lessen the time lag between provision for the project and turning the first shovel of dirt—just so does government need to do considerable thinking, in advance of the need, as to the different kinds of nonspending incentives to apply in different situations.

Our statisticians and economists—representative of business, agriculture, labor and government—certainly know enough about the problem to prepare a national full-employment budget with a considerable degree of accuracy.

In fact, ever since we began to rearm in 1940, our statisticians and economists have been projecting national budgets a year and two years ahead. These covered not only how much the nation would produce as a whole—but also how much of the total the government would need for war purposes; how much would be left over for essential civilian needs; and, of this, how much business and consumers could use for construction and other new capital expenditures. Indeed, these budget projections even made provision for certain essential items for non-belligerent allies. The Planning Committee of the War Production Board—to name but one agency—has made many such budgetary estimates. And moreover, estimating a national budget for global warfare involved venturing into new and uncharted fields, with little previous experience to guide us. But the projections worked—not on an exact basis, for the needs of global warfare, with a constantly shifting supply problem, could not be determined exactly—but they served as an essential guide to overall policy. Surely, in peacetime analysis, with a wealth of experience to draw upon, we should do an even better job.

Logistics, the science of supply, certainly can be put to work for peace as well as war—and, as I have emphasized before, within the framework of freedom.

Actually the quarterly check on the projected budget would be based upon reports to government on the investment plans of business, and upon current information on employment, consumer expenditures, and inventories. This investment information, together with reports from consumer groups, would make it possible for the

President to present to the Congress and to the country, every three months, a statement on the total number of jobs that private enterprise is currently providing and is likely to provide in the immediate future. Let us assume that a quarterly recheck showed that business investment and consumer purchases were not adding up to enough to furnish full employment. Then, it would be the immediate responsibility of the President to work out, in co-operation with business management, labor, and farm leaders, the steps and incentives necessary to bring about additional job opportunities in the various branches of industry and commerce; and, if more is required, to work out the priority in the various types of local, state, and Federal government projects which will best serve the general welfare.

If we approach the problem in this co-operative democratic way, I am sure that private enterprise and government working together can do the job. For many years we have doubled our production of goods and services every generation. I can see no reason why we should lose our ingenuity or our productive power now—with a new world of opportunities ahead. Recently, I heard a prominent English businessman say that the postwar sales talk of business should be just three words—Optimum Consumer Service. The purpose of government, then, should be to help private enterprise attain such a goal. This incentive action of government might take the form of tax reductions, broadening of credit facilities, insurances against risks not covered by normal banking arrangements, or aids in marketing, either at home or abroad. Or the government could also initiate continuing programs of useful public works to supplement and stimulate private employment. For example, by loaning money at low rates of interest for building hospitals, the government would provide many thousands of jobs, both before and after the hospital is completed.

While it is the duty of Congress, and not the President, to determine basic national policies, it is the responsibility of the President to direct the attention of Congress to situations on which Congress should make a decision. That is democracy in action. However, there is a diffusion of authority in Congress which is detrimental to legislation having a bearing on full employment—due to the fact that appropriations for programs are considered separately, by separate Congressional committees. We need joint Congressional planning. The national budget procedure I have suggested here should (a) give us co-ordinated programs submitted by the President based on available facts from both private and public sources of information, and (b) call for joint Congressional consideration by both revenue and appropriation committees. This would give more clarity to Congressional consideration and national discussion of specific current issues—on which decisions must be reached if the nation is to move swiftly and surely for full employment.

The Nature of Co-operation. In final analysis, in our democracy, the success of the national-budget approach to full employment depends upon the kind of co-operation that government can expect from business, agriculture, and labor. What is the nature of that co-operation in a free society, where we want to attain fuller and more continuous prosperity than ever before—and attain it with a maximum of private enterprise and a minimum of government activity?

For agriculture, the answer has been provided. We have now had twelve years of the most fruitful experience in agricultural co-operation with government. Farmers and farm groups work in closest collaboration with government in formulating production and price programs on a co-operative basis well in advance of the planting season. Moreover, farmers report annually what they intend to plant—and the government then prepares its forecasts of the production of crops and livestock. For twelve years now, farmers and government have worked out together various kinds of programs both to decrease or increase production, depending on the needs of the situation, to stimulate exports, to expand domestic consumption through food stamps to low-income families, to insure cotton and wheat farmers against crop losses, to aid tenants to acquire their own farm, to prevent soil erosion, to insure farmers against market losses on stored grain and cotton, and to improve farming practices generally. Thousands of county and state committeemen—all of them practical farmers— have had experience in the democratic procedure of working out production, price, and marketing programs with government. Some people, of course, had great fears in the early days; they feared they would be ultimately regimented onto collective farms. But actually, American democracy has been greatly strengthened by this co-operative

165

process. I would, therefore, anticipate no difficulties in bringing farmer co-operation to bear on the development of the agricultural part of the nation's budget.

For all business firms and organizations, the minimum of co-operation would be a willingness to supply government with information concerning inventories, orders on hand, and plans for investment expansion. We all know that many industries have excellent long-range expansion programs—particularly the A. T. & T. and other public utilities. Without divulging information to their competitors, industries, for their own intelligent planning and for the public good, should see to it that their government is kept fully informed. Without such basic data as to current trends in production—particularly up-to-date information on the extent of plans for capital investment—government cannot be expected to apply the proper incentives that might be required for different occasions.

There is, however, something more that some of our basic industries can and should do—for their own advantage, and the nation's advantage. For example, in the construction industry, the greatest contribution the various parts of the industry could make to themselves and to the general welfare would be to find the means to provide the country as a whole with a high-level, continuous volume of activity. I know that there are many obstacles to an adequate housing program on a continuous basis. These obstacles range all the way from our lack of a co-ordinated national housing program, including public and private housing, on down through adequate supplies and prices of materials, restrictions fostered by certain dealer-labor-politician combinations, and a variety of building codes that hinder more than they help. Similar obstacles must be overcome in other construction fields such as road building, and industrial and commercial construction. So far we have made very little progress toward putting the construction industry on a stable basis. But I am hopeful that once the Federal government undertakes to draw up the nation's job and production budget and co-ordinate the programs of the various groups in the housing field, the necessity for modernizing the whole construction industry would become so evident as to hasten the necessary co-operation between the labor and management groups, between management and government, and between the Federal government and our state and local governments. I know this is a large task and a great expectation. The longer we delay stimulating the necessary co-operation in this all-important field of planning, the greater the danger to our 60-million-job goal for 1950.

Business co-operation is also needed to solve another major problem—that of finding ways to put stability into capital investments for plants, equipment, inventories, office and other commercial buildings. In the past, we have had far too much bunching of business capital expenditures. When times are good, when prosperity is expected to continue, and when construction costs are expected to rise, it is quite natural for all businessmen to respond in the same hopeful way. When the boom bursts there is always the opposite mass reaction. Here is another opportunity for business statesmanship to perform an invaluable service to the whole of the economy.

For labor, as for agriculture, co-operation with government must begin with co-operation between its own organizations. It is also necessary that we have the kind of co-operation between labor and management which promotes common understanding of production, wage, and profit problems—and how the welfare of their own particular industry depends upon the welfare of the country as a whole. Most of all, we need education of union membership to make sure that the broad interests of labor are identified with those of the consumer, generally. To this end, the economic spadework of certain labor organizations in postwar planning has been highly encouraging.

In the process of developing a national budget, on the basis of current tendencies, I visualize the closest kind of co-operation between Federal agencies and the representatives of labor, management, and agriculture—so that the final recommendation submitted by the President to Congress will rest on the broadest technical and democratic base.

II

Balancing the Nation's Budget

IF BY 1950, 60 million people in the United States have jobs and are producing and consuming 200 billion dollars' worth of goods and services a year, we can be certain the nation is in a pretty fair state of economic health. We are a 200-billion-dollar nation now—and we should never be satisfied with less. To accept anything less would not be merely "Selling America Short." It would be imperiling our American heritage.

Each one of us—whether a factory worker, a farmer, a businessman, or a housewife—should know just what it means to be a 200-billion-dollar nation. For this is the measure of our economic manhood.

As consumers, we can judge what it would mean for ourselves and our families in better food, clothing, autos, homes, education, health, vacations—without that awful worry over how we are going to pay the bills. As producers we can tell what it would mean in terms of larger and steadier markets for the things we make or sell. But if we are to do our job as citizens, we must also decide what part we want business to play, and what part we want government to play, in bringing this result about.

The basic fact is, of course, that 60 million jobs cannot be maintained unless there are markets for all the things those 60 million workers can produce. Some of those markets can be provided by individual consumers in the things they buy for their own use. Some of the markets can be provided by business, in the things such as machinery and buildings that business buys for its own use. And some of the markets can be provided by government, in what government buys or uses up in maintaining public services or investing in public works.

Each one of us should form his own idea as to how much of the 200 billion dollars should be contributed by the Federal government, how much by the city and state governments, how much by consumers, and how much by businessmen. I readily admit that, at first, the process of arriving at a decision seems as complicated as trying to understand the workings of the thousand and one parts of the human system. But we don't need to know the names of the 202 bones of the body, nor do we need to understand the deep reaches of the nervous system, to know that the human body, to function best, must have proper coordination of head, heart, and stomach. Similarly, as the preceding chapter has shown, we do not need to dissect and understand every last little detail to understand how the national budget of income, expenditures, and jobs is fitted together. With not too much study, we should be able to decide whether we want to stand with those who advocate big government activity, big business activity, or big consumer activity—or some happy and democratic medium.

GETTING ON BUDGETARY SPEAKING TERMS

During the war the government has so dominated everything that all of us have felt more or less pushed around. Consider the rise in government expenditures. Back in

1929 the Federal government spent only about 4 billion dollars a year. Excluding purchases of labor and raw materials, business spent 18 billion dollars, and consumers 71 billion. Local and state governments spent about 7 billion. In other words, the Federal government represented in 1929 about four per cent of the total market of the nation for finished products. Contrast this with 1944, when the government expenditures accounted for nearly half of all the dollars spent, and the businessmen spent practically nothing for plant or equipment except at the suggestion of the government on behalf of the war effort. From the standpoint of initiating jobs, the Federal government in 1944 was more than twenty times as important as in 1929.

I believe that we can have a national budget of 200 billion dollars and 60 million jobs by 1950—and balance our Federal budget at the same time. Furthermore, I believe that we can attain these three objectives in several different ways. But before going into these different ways I should like to call attention to Table II, which is taken from Franklin Roosevelt's last budget message. This is the same as Table I we considered in the previous chapter, except here 1944 is shown as well as 1939. Table II illustrates in the simplest way possible the extraordinary change which took place in the Federal government budget relative to the nation's budget during the war. It might be said to be a variation of the old theme of the popular song, "The Music Goes 'Round and 'Round and Comes Out Here." It will stand a lot of pondering. For with a few figures it tells us many fundamental facts.

The table not only points up the tremendous increase in national income, but it also shows how differently the income was used. In 1939, consumers spent 62 billion of the total of 90 billion dollars for their own purposes—while the Federal government spent only 9 billion. In 1944, consumers spent only 98 billion of the 200-billion-dollar total for themselves—while the Federal government spent 96 billions. In addition, consumers' savings were enormously increased.

The part of their income which consumers and businesses save gets into use only when it is borrowed and spent. Some is borrowed by other businesses and spent to build houses, plants, and equipment—or is borrowed by cities, states, or the Federal government and spent for public improvements. In 1939, borrowing by local, state, and Federal governments to the extent of 3 billion dollars accounted for only about half of consumers' savings—while business invested all its own savings and also borrowed the other half (2.6 billion) of consumers' savings. In 1944, on the contrary, the Federal government, spending enormous sums for war, borrowed all of the 37 billions of consumers' savings, all of the 9 billions of business savings, and all of the 2 billions of state and local government savings—in addition to raising far greater sums through taxes.

Getting on speaking terms with the nation's budget is as difficult as getting on living terms with a simple budget in one's own home. But it is another of our necessary chores if we are to have the intelligent public opinion so essential to our progress. We are going to hear a lot about the nation's budget from now on—so we should try to grasp the component parts, brought together in Table II, which follows on pages 174-5.

As we study Table II we begin to perceive how the Federal budget might have been balanced in 1944. We could have put such heavy taxes on consumers that they would have had no savings. To do that, we would have had to tax ourselves, as private citizens, about three times as heavily as we were taxed. Or we could have taxed all the undistributed profits and reserves of business, which would have meant a business tax about one and a half times as high as we had in 1944. I am not saying we should have levied these heavier taxes; I am merely showing where the money could have come from if Congress had decided to finance the war entirely on a pay-as-you-go basis.

In the peace to come, we are not going to have either a national budget or a Federal budget which looks like either the 1939 column or the 1944 column in Table II. The Federal government is not going to spend anywhere near as much as 96 billion dollars in time of peace—nor is it going to spend as little as 9 billion dollars. Exactly what the Federal government will spend must still be determined by the appropriate authorities in Congress, acting upon the President's recommendation. But we shall have to spend about 6 billion dollars a year in interest charges on the Federal debt. That's the first item. Then, we shall probably have to spend around 4 billion dollars annually to take care of services of various kinds for around 15 million veterans. And to maintain our armed services in a high state of efficiency will cost us several billions more at least for the first few years after the war. Add in something for agricultural aid, for raising the standard of housing, health, and nutrition, for aid to education, and for the

TABLE II. THE FEDERAL BUDGET AND

Calendar years 1939 and 1944

ECONOMIC GROUP

CONSUMERS
Income after taxes
Expenditures

Savings (+)

BUSINESS
Undistributed profits and reserves
Gross capital formation

Excess of receipts (+) or capital formation (—)

STATE AND LOCAL GOVERNMENTS
Receipts from the public, other than borrowing
Payments to the public

Excess of receipts (+) or payments (—)

FEDERAL GOVERNMENT
Receipts from the public, other than borrowing
Payments to the public

Excess of receipts (+) or payments (—)

Less: Adjustments [2]

TOTAL: GROSS NATIONAL PRODUCT
Receipts
Expenditures

                 * Balance

THE NATION'S BUDGET

(current prices [1] in billions)

Calendar year 1939			Calendar year 1944		
Receipts	Expenditures	Excess (+) Deficit (—)	Receipts	Expenditures	Excess (+) Deficit (—)
$67.3			$134.5		
	$61.7			$ 97.6	
		+$5.6			+$36.9
$ 8.3			$ 10.6		
	$10.9			$ 1.8	
		—$2.6			+$ 8.8
$ 8.9			$ 10.1		
	$ 9.1			$ 8.3	
		—$0.2			+$ 1.8
$ 6.5			$ 48.1		
	$ 9.3			$ 95.6	
		—$2.8			—$47.5
$ 2.4	$ 2.4		$ 4.6	$ 4.6	
$88.6			$198.7		
	$88.6			$198.7	
		* 0			* 0

[1] Prices in 1944 were between 25 and 30 per cent above 1939.
[2] Mainly government expenditures for other than goods and services.

regular functions of the Federal government, and we would have a total of upwards of 20 billion dollars—perhaps closer to 25 billion dollars. This for the Federal government alone.

For employment, 1929 was a pretty good year—with less than 2 million people unemployed. Allowing for normal growth, how would the 1929 national budget look in 1950? To convert 1929 into 1950, about all we have to do is to double the total figure. And we have good precedent for doing this—for not only are we still a rapidly growing nation; but, as we have already noted, we have doubled our physical production of goods and services every generation. Valued in 1944 prices, the goods and services we produced in 1890 were worth about 25 billion dollars; in 1910, about 50 billion dollars; and in 1929, about 100 billion dollars. To live up to our potentialities in the future as we have in the past would mean 200 billion dollars by 1949–1950. Because of all-out war production, we reached a 200-billion-dollar total national product in 1944—six years ahead of time. There may well be some sag-back in 1946 and 1947—but if we are to keep up with our past record of growth we should be up to 200 billion dollars again in 1950.

JUST WHERE DOES A BUDGET BALANCE?

Let us disregard at this point the kind of national budget we shall need for the immediate reconversion period, and consider only the budgetary choices ahead of us—the ways we can have a balanced Federal budget, plus 60 million jobs and a national income of 200 billion dollars, by 1950.

Table III illustrates some of these choices. At this distance, of course, we cannot predict the special or temporary circumstances that the nation's budget for 1950 would need to meet. Instead, the budget models in Table III deliberately show certain abnormally excessive expenditures by one group, thus illustrating the problem inherent in that particular model, and emphasizing the fact that we must not fix our minds on any particular set of figures as being unchangeable. After all, the function of budgeting is to strike a balance between abnormalities on a basis that will assure the greatest productivity and the highest standard of living.

TABLE III. NATIONAL BUDGETS FOR 60 MILLION JOBS
(billion dollars)

NATIONAL BUDGETS	Spent by Consumers	Spent by Business for Capital Formation[1]	Spent by Gov't, Federal, State, Local	Total
1929 (Actual)	71	18	11	100
1944 (Actual)	97	3	98	198
1950 Models: (1944 prices)				
1929 Model	142	36	22	200
Government Model	120	15	65	200
Business Model	130	35	35	200
Consumer Model	140	25	35	200
Consumer-Business Model	135	30	35	200

[1] Includes chiefly expenditures for plant and equipment, residential and other private construction and net exports of goods.

Of the four 1950 models listed in Table III, I don't like the "government model" and "1929 model." They are too extreme. In the case of the "government model," with con-

BUDGETS FOR A 200 BILLION DOLLAR
NATIONAL PRODUCTION

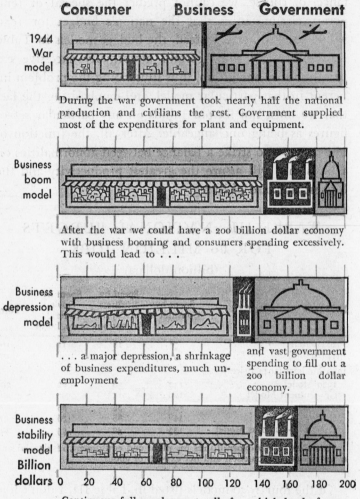

Consumer   Business   Government

1944
War
model

During the war government took nearly half the national production and civilians the rest. Government supplied most of the expenditures for plant and equipment.

Business
boom
model

After the war we could have a 200 billion dollar economy with business booming and consumers spending excessively. This would lead to . . .

Business
depression
model

. . . a major depression, a shrinkage of business expenditures, much unemployment

and vast government spending to fill out a 200 billion dollar economy.

Business
stability
model
**Billion
dollars** 0   20   40   60   80   100   120   140   160   180   200

Continuous full employment calls for a high level of consumer spending. Of the total budget, consumers would spend about two-thirds and the rest would be divided between business and government.

sumers spending only 120 billion and business only 15 billion dollars, we would have 10 million or more unemployed if government spent only 30 billion; but there would be no unemployment if government spent the entire balance of 65 billions. Every practical person, in and out of politics, however, knows that neither the people nor Congress would tolerate the heavy taxes or continuously soaring public debt that would accompany such expenditures in time of peace. On the other hand, the "1929 model," based on the minimum of expenditure by government and the maximum by business and consumers, might be very popular for a time. But it just won't do for two very practical reasons. In the first place we are, of necessity, going to have a combined Federal, state, and local government budget considerably in excess of 22 billions. In the second place, it is too top-heavy with business expenditures. It reflects a boomtime overexpansion in capital goods which would lead inevitably to another bustup like that of 1929 or worse.

Our choice, therefore, lies really between the "business model" and the "consumer model." The former still emphasizes business expenditures, while the latter exaggerates consumer expenditures. The "business model" calls for capital expenditures practically as heavy as we found in the overexaggerated "1929 model." If businessmen put too large an investment into plant and equipment, or into inventories, there must be additional consumer purchasing power to support it. I rather like the so-called "consumer model" which calls for consumers spending 140 billion dollars in 1950, or about 40 billion dollars more than they actually spent in 1944. Under this assumption, both business and government expenditures would be greater than in previous peacetime years. While this is not unreasonable if we take into account the normal growth of the country, its rising living standards and the necessary larger postwar expenditures by both, it could lead to instability if consumers spend disproportionately in any year or two on durable goods instead of on goods and services that need to be purchased continuously. For this reason it may be wiser and more realistic to aim at a balance somewhere between the business and consumer models—the "consumer-business model," the last item in Table III.

These forms of the national budget are only preliminary samples. The whole idea is new and still rapidly developing. For instance, it is probable that we shall need to show the effect of "transfer" payments more fully, such as life insurance, and the sale and repayment of E bonds, which account for billions of savings that do not appear in the "net" figure. For the present, it is the need for a clear national accounting—not the exact form—that should be kept uppermost in mind.

I do not think we have examined and discussed the national budgeting problem sufficiently as yet to say just where the balance point is between consumer purchasing power and business productivity. For the present, I am inclined to think we may get the greatest progress if we aim to have consumers supply about two-thirds of the 200 billion dollars of national expenditure—and the balance about equally divided between business and government expenditures. But I am certain that it is at this point that the highest quality of national statesmanship is required and demanded of leaders in government, business and labor, and agriculture. The wisdom shown at this point will have much to do with determining whether we are to have full employment or mass unemployment all over again.

THE NEED FOR FLEXIBILITY

We have concerned ourselves up to now chiefly with speculation regarding budget choices for a period beginning several years after the war. There are some observations, both with regard to business and consumer expenditures, that we need to make with regard to the immediate reconversion period.

In both business and consumer expenditures during the reconversion period, we cannot depend upon any stable situations. This means that our thinking about the business-consumer-government parts of the national budget during the reconversion must be kept quite flexible, so as to be more adjustable to the changing needs of our national productive machinery.

With regard to business expenditure for plant and equipment we shall undoubtedly find that considerable expansion will be required to assure our goal of a high level of consumption. The Federal government spent around 16 billion dollars for war production facilities. But I very much doubt if more than a third of this new capacity can be converted to profitable peacetime production. Moreover, day and night operation has caused excessive depreciation of all our industrial plants—making heavy replacements imperative. Much time will be consumed, and special provisions may be required, in acquiring the new equipment and replacements so necessary in attaining the

A 200 BILLION DOLLAR
NATIONAL BUDGET

As a nation of producers this is
how we divide the income we
receive:

As a nation of consumers this is
how we distribute our spending:

Wages and salaries 110	Food, drink & tobacco
	Other goods & services
	Rent & household goods
	Clothing
Income of proprietors 27 Farm operators & unin- corporated businesses	Transportation
Corporate profits 18 After taxes	**Business investment** Homes, plant. equipment, inventories, net exports
Rents, royalties, interest . dividends 15	
Corporate & business taxes 20	**Government** Federal, state & local
Depreciation & reserves 10	

Total gross national product 200
Billion
dollars

200 Total expenditures
Billion
dollars

200-billion-dollar standard of living by 1950. But if we are operating under the benefits of the national-budget approach to full employment, these changing needs and conditions—and the issues that go with them—can be more easily crystallized for general consideration by the private and public interests involved, and appropriate action recommended and taken.

Similarly, we face a serious problem in consumer expenditures in the reconversion and beyond. There is real danger that consumers, in the first few years after civilian production restrictions are lifted, will draw too heavily upon wartime savings in their eagerness to buy houses, automobiles, refrigerators, washing machines, and other things denied them during the war—the danger that they will stampede for the nearest store entrance to buy things that did not need replacement, simply for the sake of buying. In other words, while we are reconverting to peace-time production and consumption, we shall have to consider what would happen if there are four or five years of overspending by consumers, followed by four or five years of lack of consumer demand. We must find a way to regularize purchases of durable consumer goods, and at the same time, to broaden expenditures for nondurable goods and services such as food, clothing, health, education, and recreation, to live better and spend more on living better.

THE NATION'S BUDGET AND TAXES

Of uppermost importance in balancing the parts of the nation's budget is Federal taxation—and in formulating our postwar tax policy we must exercise the utmost care,

(1) to find the proper means of levying taxes so as to provide the maximum stimulation to national production; and (2) to protect the public interest from those who would seek special tax privilege.

Although we can afford to tax less severely in peace than in war, we shall still need to collect for the Federal, state and local governments a total of around 35 billion dollars. And as the Federal government needs around 25 billion dollars of the total, the way this huge sum is collected will affect directly the spending of consumers and the activity of business.

All of us, therefore, can stand more familiarity with the meaning of taxes. We need to know how taxes were used during the war, how they affect the purchasing power of consumers, how they can be used to stimulate small and big business investment, and how they may be used to help check inflation or deflation. I'm not proposing, by any means, to go into all the intricacies of taxation. But to talk about balancing the nation's budget without introducing taxes would be like Dickens' *Christmas Carol* without Scrooge—or *Uncle Tom's Cabin* without Simon Legree.

Under war conditions, drastic use of the taxing power was essential to prevent inflation and to help meet the enormous cost of war. During the war the Federal government multiplied its taxes more than seven times. It taxed incomes heavily, and it encouraged everyone to buy War Bonds so as to lessen the danger caused by too much purchasing power and not enough civilian goods. In addition, it imposed a heavy excess-profits tax on corporations and provided for a renegotiation of war contracts so as to limit war profits. Without exceedingly heavy wartime taxes and other controls, the cost of living would have skyrocketed—and the profits of business would have been so large as to destroy the judgment of all but the very wise.

Without heavy wartime taxes we could not have mobilized our entire economy for a total war effort. I am not arguing that our wartime tax policy has been perfect; the pressures at play in a democracy make perfection most difficult to achieve. I know, too, that too many people have made too much money out of this war. But I am also sure that our wartime tax policy demonstrates that we profited considerably from past experience; and that it also contributed mightily to a record of war administration which —particularly considering the nature and extent of the opposition, both personal and political—is, indeed, a record of remarkable accomplishment.

In attaining the necessary maximum of peacetime production, the primary task of the Federal government in formulating tax policy is the levying of taxes in such a way as to give a maximum of encouragement to private enterprise—and still avoid putting an unfair burden upon the middle- and low-income groups. To do this demands a minimum of political compromise.

As for general tax policy, we should remember that every reduction we make in direct consumption taxes will be reflected, almost dollar for dollar, in an increase in what the consumer buys. This applies particularly to the sales tax, which imposes too heavy a tax burden upon the lower-income groups. But it also applies to a wide variety of levies, such as wartime utility taxes and wartime excise taxes on a multitude of commodities.

Undoubtedly, it would be a tremendous stimulant to business activity to abolish the excess-profits tax at the earliest possible moment after the war is over and the danger of inflation is past. This excess-profits tax was essential in wartime. But suppose in peacetime that as much as eighty cents out of every dollar of profit went to the Federal government in taxes; certainly, many corporations would not operate as efficiently as they should to contribute their share to our total national production. The excess-profits tax, therefore, should be ended as rapidly as possible so that business will be stimulated to reconvert with the greatest speed possible. Moreover, the rapidity of refunds from the excess-profits tax means much to small businesses which are cramped for credit. But the broad objective in modifying the excess-profits tax—the objective of the general welfare—must be to encourage the maximum of those peacetime investments that were postponed because of the war, and are now needed for full employment in peace.

Some experts in tax policy believe that the best possible incentive to business would be to erase all ordinary peacetime profit taxes from the statutes—and to levy taxes only on corporation dividends, on individual incomes, and on consumption. But these people overlook the simple fact that not all profits are distributed as dividends—and that not all undistributed profits go into job-creating investment. It could well be that some corporations, for a time, would be so stimulated as to expand their investment in plant and equipment—and also to increase their dividends. But even this would be a very shortsighted advantage. It would mean that consumers would be carrying the entire tax burden—and they would have their overall purchasing power reduced to much the same extent that the tax burden was passed back upon them. Instead, I think we must seek a balance between taxing business and the consumers. We need to stimulate business, yes—but we need also to protect the consumers who buy the products of business. This is the balance that is called for in the business-consumer model of the nation's budget.

THE USE OF TAX CONCESSIONS

Among the inducements for risk-taking, I would recommend a modification in the corporate tax system so that business can get proper credit for losses. Too many businessmen have had to pay income taxes on every dollar of profit—but have found it impossible to get credit for their losses. Some of these businessmen, especially after they have passed the age of fifty, say in their despair: "The dice are loaded against me. What's the use? I'm not in business for my health." And so they retire before they should.

Corporation taxes can be used not only as a device for stimulating business in general, but they can and must be used also in behalf of small corporations that do not enjoy certain advantages possessed by large corporations. I believe we should differentiate between those concerns which have access to the national capital markets (stock exchanges and over-the-counter markets) or who sell their obligations to insurance companies or other financial institutions and those who, because of their small size, do not have the advantage of these nation-wide sources of capital and must pay higher interest rates to their local bankers. These small corporations must rely on more costly private sources of financing. The activity of these smaller companies would be greatly stimulated, I am sure, if they were to be given the option of being taxed as partnerships instead of as corporations. This would mean a lot to small growing businesses which want to plow back most of their profits into tangible capital investment. And it would help to put small businesses into a better competitive position. Small corporations don't want charity—but they would like to have, and deserve to have, present inequities corrected.

Of course, this concession would have to be worked out in such a way that large corporations could not take unfair advantage of it.

There is another tax question that directly affects business, individuals, and the Federal part of the nation's budget. This is the social-security payroll tax paid by both employer and employees. I long have advocated extension of social-security coverage to include everyone. But I doubt the wisdom of meeting the additional benefits by greatly increased payroll taxes. To avoid the deflationary effect of heavy payroll taxes, I believe that a substantial part of the costs of social security should be paid for out of the regular Federal budget—that is, out of general taxation—and, in order to maintain purchasing power, we should also be prompt in lowering the rates on the rest of the tax at the first sign of a business recession. Everyone's contribution to social security would be more nearly in line with his capacity to pay if the contribution were made through general taxation rather than through high payroll taxes.

Taxes have an even greater balancing function when we face dangers of inflation or deflation—when purchasing power in the national budget is likely either to exceed or fall short of the available supply of goods.

When purchasing power exceeds the supply of goods, we should seek to hold public expenditures to the minimum necessary to maintain essential public services. And if the inflation danger were serious—as it would be if too many people tried to spend too much of their wartime savings too fast—we could also raise income taxes. The reduced expenditures and increased tax receipts would produce a Federal surplus, which could then be used to reduce the public debt. The balancing job in an inflationary period would be that of reducing both the government share and the consumer share of the national budget, and using the reduction of debt as an inflation preventive. But in times of threatened deflation, with a decline in business spending, we would seek to expand both the government and the consumer shares of the nation's budget.

Once the danger of a serious postwar inflation is passed, then we must give prompt attention to tax reductions. Never again in our lifetime shall we have a tax bill as low as that of 1939 or 1940. However, with a 200-billion-dollar full-employment situation, we could have a tax bill about half of that of 1945. We can't count on anything lower than that. As I noted earlier in this chapter, this would be sufficient for a Federal postwar budget adding up to be-

tween 20 and 25 billion dollars. Then, with the full co-
operation of business, labor, and agriculture in achieving
and maintaining full employment—thereby guaranteeing a
minimum of government spending—we can approach, with
lighter heart and heavier purse, the retirement of the national debt.

III

The Low Cost of Full Employment

COUNTLESS PEOPLE tell me: "Of course we should have
full employment, but how can we afford it? I'm for
60 million jobs, but who is going to pay the bill? We shall
come out of this war with a debt of over 300 billion dollars
—and if the people insist that government take on the responsibility for 60 million job opportunities, we shall go
bankrupt. Remember, the Federal budget will have to provide 6 billion dollars a year for interest on the debt—4 or 5
billion dollars a year to take care of the veterans—somewhere between 5 and 10 billion dollars a year to maintain
a much larger peacetime army and navy than we ever before envisioned—and perhaps from 3 to 4 billion for the
normal services of the government. Even without provision for public works and participation in the development of our resources—and without any provision for Federal aid to health, housing and education—this would be a

minimum of 18 billion dollars and a maximum of 25 billion dollars a year. We just simply can't take on the risk of
a continuously high tax burden and government borrowing to assure 60 million jobs. Already the Federal debt
comes to over $2000 per person. No, I'm sorry, but we
mustn't abuse our national credit any more."

While this attitude would seem to rest on good logic,
actually, it is basically wrong. It demands, however, the
best answer we can give. For if enough well-intentioned
people hold this view, the fuller and more secure life that
lies ahead for all of us cannot be attained—because this
attitude rests upon a fear of our 300-billion-dollar debt
that is so exaggerated that it may quite possibly block the
way to 60 million jobs and the necessary 200-billion-dollar
national peacetime production to guarantee those jobs.

Let me meet this fear in several ways. First, let's make
sure we understand one basic fact—that just as mass unemployment means huge dollar costs to the nation, full employment means low costs. Taking a chance on national
co-operation for full employment could not possibly even
approach the costs we undoubtedly would have to pay if
we took another chance with mass unemployment. Surely,
we have learned that lesson—the terribly hard way. Once
we begin compromising with the sum total of our needs—
once we begin to believe that somehow we shall get along
indefinitely with 5 million or 10 million unemployed workers—then we are accepting a process that can only bring us
to economic ruin. We shall be forcing the nation's sights
down from a 200-billion-dollar national production to 125
billion dollars—consumer purchasing power from 135 to

80 billion dollars—corporation gross profits from 25 billion to less than 5 billion dollars—and farm cash income from 22 billion to a mere 7 billion dollars. Mass unemployment again would force huge Federal expenditures. And the Federal budget again would be heavily unbalanced. This is what is bound to happen all over again if we keep on fooling ourselves.

The low cost of full employment is the opposite of all this. We could cut tax collections almost in half and still provide more Federal aid for health, housing, education, and social security than before the war—if by 1950 we have 60 million people at work producing 200 billion dollars' worth of goods and services. Business profits would be large enough to keep industry in a state of healthy expansion—with wage rises keeping pace with the increase in productivity, and farm cash income remaining close to its present high level.

Some people, evidently to console themselves in their stubborn opposition to progress, have the queer notion that Franklin Roosevelt came out for 60 million jobs simply as an excuse for government spending more money. No sane statesman wants to increase the Federal debt if it can possibly be avoided. It is just because we must not increase the debt burden that I have emphasized the ways to avoid it—the many ways of stimulating employment in private enterprise with a minimum of government spending and a maximum of co-operation. What many people do not yet realize is that with a world needing to be rebuilt, with job opportunities beckoning from every undeveloped corner of the United States and from every research laboratory, the great bulk of the 60 million jobs would be provided by private initiative. For these people, I want to emphasize that the success of any government program, in terms of low cost, depends on government stimulating private industry by taxation, credit, foreign trade, and other devices to such an extent that Federal, state, and local government will not have to carry more than the approximately 17 per cent of the load shown in the business-consumer budget model—or 35 billion dollars a year. With full employment conditions, the Federal government would not need to spend any more than this of the people's money to stimulate free enterprise by participating in developing our resources, and in aiding health, housing, and education, to foster new inventions, to facilitate foreign trade, and, by providing necessary credit, to foster the maximum of competitive use in new technological devices—to provide these and other services in addition to operating its regular departmental functions. And even when government stimulates the economy with public construction, the jobs for the most part would be provided by private firms under government contract.

But the important thing is not that the government should always be seeking to sponsor a vast amount of activity of this kind—but rather that both business and the consumers should know that government has the plans all blueprinted and ready for use should the need arise. The certainty that government has been provided with the power to prevent unemployment should give business the courage to carry most of the burden of full employment itself—and thus help keep government spending down. It would be true economy for Congress to appropriate at once at least a hundred million dollars for the purpose of blueprinting public projects now to provide this sense of security. This amount may seem large—but actually the public projects that could be blueprinted for this sum would total only about 3 billion dollars. But this would be enough to give us a good start along the right road.

CO-OPERATION: THE PRICE OF BALANCE

In proposing the nation's budget as a businesslike system for avoiding the high cost of unemployment, I have suggested that greater stability undoubtedly would be attained if we strove for a balance between the consumer and business types of budget—bearing in mind, of course, that in any one year the circumstances of any given situation will dictate the best combination of the parts. In a consumer-business budget of a national production of 200 billion dollars, the Federal contribution would be about 25 billions, the contribution of state and local government might be about 10 billions, and the balance of 165 billions would be consumer and business expenditures—approximating 135 billion dollars for consumers and 30 billion dollars for business. Such a combination would readily yield the 25 billions of the Federal taxes sufficient to cover the necessary Federal outlays. There would be no additions to the Federal debt if business and consumer expenditures were kept at a combined level of 165 billion dollars. But let's not fool ourselves by this low cost arithmetic. We shall not be able to keep costs of full employment down to the minimum represented by a Federal budget balanced at between 20 to 25 billion dollars without paying the necessary price in co-operative effort.

In striving for this co-operation, special emphasis must be placed on the capital-investment side of the nation's budget—in getting the proper kind of prompt co-operative action on housing and health programs, on urban and rural development, on the construction industry generally, on business investment in new plants, and on the building up of exports and imports. These, in broad outline, are the fields in which the maximum of co-operation is required to maintain the maximum of business investment and consumer expenditure to guarantee a minimum of Federal expenditures.

The price for this maximum of business investment and consumer expenditure *must* be paid by a willingness to co-operate—and not by an increase in the Federal debt. This demands a maximum of co-operation every step of the way between Main Street and Washington—between Congressional and Senate appropriation and revenue committees; between the House and Senate; between the Congress and the President; between the various departments and agencies of the Federal government, and between Federal, state, and local governments; between government and business, labor and agriculture; and between management and labor. I feel sure that if we would only fear the Federal debt less and fear more the consequences of our failure to achieve this co-operation, then we would have full employment at a low cost to the taxpayer—and with full employment, and only with full employment, we would have such a balance in the Federal budget that would allow us steadily to lighten the burden of the Federal debt.

When I began to write this book, I began to think as much about the problem of the national debt as about full employment—and so I did a little "boning up" on history. And in one of the volumes of Lord Macaulay, I found a discussion of the British debt, up to and through the Napoleonic wars, which is applicable to our own national position today. It gives us a timely bit of debt perspective. Therefore, I think it is very much worth quoting here, and it will be remembered, of course, that the medium of exchange is not the dollar but the pound sterling:

> At every stage in the growth of that debt the nation has set up the same cry of anguish and despair. At every stage in the growth of that debt it has been seriously asserted by wise men that bankruptcy and ruin were at hand. Yet still the debt went on growing; and still bankruptcy and ruin were as remote as ever. When the great contest with Louis XIV was finally terminated by the peace of Utrecht, the nation owed about fifty millions; and that debt was considered . . . by acute and profound thinkers as an incumbrance which would permanently cripple the body politic. Nevertheless, trade flourished; wealth increased; the nation became richer and richer. Then came the War of the Austrian Succession; and the debt rose to eighty millions.
>
> Pamphleteers, historians, and orators pronounced that now, at all events, our case was desperate. . . . Soon war again broke forth; and under the energetic administration of the First William Pitt, the debt rapidly swelled to a hundred and forty millions; . . . men of theory and

196

men of business almost unanimously pronounced that the fatal day had now really arrived. . . . Not less gloomy was the view which George Grenville, a minister eminently diligent and practical, took of our financial situation. The nation must, he conceived, sink under a debt of a hundred and forty millions, unless a portion of the load were borne by the American Colonies. The attempt to lay a portion of the load on the American Colonies produced another war. That war left us with an additional hundred millions of debt, and without the Colonies whose help had been represented as indispensable. . . . Soon, however, the wars which sprang from the French Revolution . . . tasked the powers of public credit to the utmost. When the world was again at rest the funded debt of England amounted to eight hundred millions. . . . It was in truth a gigantic, a fabulous debt; and we can hardly wonder that the cry of despair should have been louder than ever. But again that cry was found to have been as unreasonable as ever. After a few years of exhaustion, England recovered herself. Yet like Addison's valetudinarian, who continued to whimper that he was dying of consumption till he became so fat that he was shamed into silence, she went on complaining that she was sunk in poverty till her wealth showed itself by tokens which made her complaints ridiculous. The beggared, the bankrupt society not only proved able to meet all its obligations, but while meeting those obligations, grew richer and richer so fast that the growth could almost be discerned by the eye. . . .

The prophets of evil were under a double delusion. They erroneously imagined that there was an exact analogy between the case of an individual who is in debt to another individual and the case of a society which is in debt to a part of itself. . . . They made no allowance for the effect produced by the incessant progress of every experimental science, and by the incessant efforts of every man to get on in life. They saw that the debt grew; and they forgot that other things grew as well as the debt.

We, too, live in an age of incessant progress—and the horizon is much brighter with opportunity than Lord Macaulay possibly could have envisioned for his England of a century ago. We, too, have benefited by the "incessant efforts of every man to get on in life." This is recorded for us in the fact that every twenty years we have managed to double our national production of the things we want and need to have. It was the equivalent of 50 billion in 1909, and 100 billion in 1929. It can be 200 billion in 1949—and, I dare to say, it can reach 400 billion in 1969 if private enterprise will only live up to its profitable opportunity of providing a fuller life for all of us.

PART SIX

The Fuller Life for All

WE AMERICANS are at our best when we have a hard job to do. The bigger the job is the better we do it —provided that the purpose is clearly defined. When we are thus challenged we plan better, work harder, and produce more than any other people who have ever lived on this earth. Starting with practically an empty arsenal in 1940, we created the most powerful military machine the world has ever seen. In peace, too, we have achieved similar industrial miracles. We must never forget that the genius of America has always been best expressed by the four simple words—"All things are possible." And to me, the greatest miracle of all has always been the casual way we take our miracles for granted.

We went all-out for war. We never faltered. We lived up to our capacities. We "measured ourselves against history." In the peace to come, the American spirit now demands that we go all out to win the People's Peace—that we make full use of all manpower, all natural resources, all technologies, all inventions, and all business-management capacities, to produce the maximum quantity of those things which the American people need and must have year after year. The peace, too, demands that we live up to our capacities.

I am willing to grant that with only 5 million people at work—and with all of the rest of us somehow living upon the slavery of those 5 million—it would be possible to furnish the American people with a higher standard of living than that enjoyed by the Hindus. And I am further willing to grant that with only 50 million people at work, it would be possible for the American people for a time to enjoy a higher standard of living than any other nation in the world—though I wonder how long the Federal debt and our free-enterprise system could stand the forces of economic disintegration which the continued lack of full employment would bring. But neither the "poorest" nor the "possibly fair" will suffice when the "best" can be had. Out of this war must come the determination to work, produce, live and play abundantly. That applies to all of us —not to just the few.

The material basis of the fuller life for all which every person in the United States craves and deserves—if he is willing to work for it—is the simple basis of food, clothing, shelter, and the opportunity easily and cheaply to move himself and his property from place to place. Almost on a par with these four fundamentals, most Americans will put communications—whether by publication, radio, movie, or wire. Day by day—even hour by hour—we want to know exactly what is going on in the world. But in order really to appreciate this material basis to the fullest extent we must have education to give us a fundamental grasp of the hard realities of history, geography, economics, and politics.

I cannot disassociate these ultimate aspects of the good life from the fundamentals of food and clothing, housing and transportation, communications and education.

The science of nutrition has made such great gains in the past fifteen years that not one person in a thousand even begins to grasp the extent to which life can be enriched by proper diet. The farmers can easily produce abundant quantities of the right kind of food, provided only that all of the consumers have productive jobs. But both the farmers and the consumers must allow themselves to be guided to some extent by those findings of the scientific nutritionists which point the way toward health and efficiency.

There was a time when I approached the problem of eating in much the same spirit as an automobile driver asking the filling-station attendant to fill up the tank with any kind of gasoline. But as I have studied more deeply the science of nutrition, and especially as I have traveled around the world and have become familiar with the cooking in many lands and of many peoples, I have also come to appreciate the art as well as the science of food. I respect and admire most of the true gourmets I have met. Their shapes often may be globular and their movements slow— but their judgment is usually wise and their opinion sound. I can only ask that they not forget that for too many people in this country, where food is concerned, abundance comes before the art of appreciation.

Personally, in the matter of clothing, I have never aspired to the sartorial perfection of, say, my good friends Sumner Welles and Rexford Tugwell. But as I have grown older—and as I have given more and more thought to people's habits—I have come to realize just how much the mere possession of an extra good suit or a street dress can mean to the psychological health of men and women. People say I am addicted to all kinds of statistics. Perhaps so—and so I will venture the flat statement that 99 44/100 of all husbands want to see their wives well dressed. Speaking as a husband, I suppose I shall never quite understand what it is that makes one strange type of woman's hat so chic one year and so dowdy the next. But that has nothing to do with the basic right of every woman to beautify herself in any way she may desire. However, I should also like to offer another figure—this one quite real.

The average family in the United States, before the war, could afford to .pend only about a hundred and fifty dollars a year for clothing. That's not much, considering all the demands upon the family purse. Those much-wanted Sunday clothes, that extra pair of pants for the boy, or that graduation dress for the girl—these are far from being small items of consideration in even an average budget. Surely, in such a land of potential abundance as ours, it should not be too much to expect that even the lowest-income families could buy at least three hundred dollars' worth of clothes a year.

In housing, we have already seen how far we still have to go in providing a fuller life for all. The peasant of northwestern Europe, before the war, usually lived in a better house than the American farmer, and was more likely to have rural electrification—although the American farmer often had the best of it with regard to power machinery. With all our ingenuity, we haven't yet learned to build good cheap houses in the same way that we have learned to build good cheap refrigerators and automobiles. This challenge to our fuller life is one for our immediate postwar acceptance.

In communications between people, including our transportation from place to place, we more nearly live the full life than any other people in the world. Our average family travels more miles than the average family in any other country. Yet, compared with what it ought to be, our transportation system still is only fair. Too many railroads have been slow in keeping up with new forms of competition; all too often they have used their pressure to stifle competition. In a postwar life of full employment, we shall need to have the fullest competition among railways, highways, waterways, and airways so as to get the maximum in service at the minimum of cost. This will call for increased government assistance to highways, airports, and waterways—the same kind of assistance the government gave to the railroads in their early years.

Anyone who has driven along the Pennsylvania Turnpike or along one of the other multilane highways—where all the towns are bypassed and all the crossroads are overpasses or underpasses—knows the tremendous savings in time which such modern highways offer to the automobile driver who, whether on business or out for recreation, must drive long distances safely in a short space of time. In the fuller postwar life we shall need the rapid expansion of these superhighways—just as we shall need a nationwide system of modern airports to facilitate the development of private flying. Actually, I look forward to the not-too-distant day when the private aviation enthusiast will be able to fly his own light plane from Buenos Aires to Alaska, with airports spaced every few hundred miles along the way.

This expansion in transportation facilities will make it

easier to attain the fuller life of recreation which we all want to enjoy and should be able to enjoy—remembering, too, the material importance of recreation in our economy. Recreation is already the leading industry in several New England states as well as in Florida, and in whole areas of California, Wisconsin, Minnesota, Michigan, and the Rockies. More than a million people in the United States make their living directly or indirectly out of servicing the seasonal boarder, the family on an automobile tour, or the week-end recreationist. All fields of recreation will be greatly expanded with full employment—and this expansion will more or less parallel the expansion in transportation facilities.

Many people dislike recreation in any form. Personally, I think that recreation is almost as important to the good life as food, shelter, clothing, and transportation. Why shouldn't man work in order to have a good time? Why shouldn't he work in order to have a summer home for his family and a good car to enable him to visit that family over the week-end? Why shouldn't he work in order to enjoy his week-end golf or fishing trip? Why shouldn't every man and woman, every boy and girl, have the time and means to enjoy his or her own form of recreation or sport—his or her hobby? Recreation gives a broader outlook on life. It trains our bodies and spirits in the give and take of daily comradeship. To live abundantly demands more emphasis on recreation of all kinds in the future than in the past—and for all the people. We have the manpower and the resources to enable every one of us to live a fuller life. Why don't we do it?

In the final analysis the full life is a thing of the spirit. It is a matter of ideas and ideals—of both education and religion. The purpose of education and religion is to open both to ourselves and to the next generation the paths of deeper, more thoughtful and more fruitful living.

Religion contributes to teaching man to take a larger view of life—to thinking about *why* we do things instead of *how* to do them. Every great religious leader has worked for the general welfare—for the issues of social progress in his time, and against those who "ground down the faces of the poor." Down through the centuries, the basic emphasis on social and human values has remained as the great contribution of religion.

Education supplements the religious ideal by making us more efficient in acquiring material, intellectual, and spiritual possessions. Education must give us and our children an understanding of all the sciences of man, and a background of history, geography, economics, and government — so that we and our children may live in harmony among ourselves at home and with all nations abroad. It is important to educate for the fullest use of our resources and skills. But it is even more important to educate for character—the kind of character which enables us to get along in a decent, humane, and co-operative way.

We must educate our children not only to make a success in life as competitive individuals—but also, and even more important, to work together in the service of the general welfare. In recent years, education has placed so much emphasis on the individual, and so little on the general welfare, that both government and business have become more and more a battleground of selfish pressure groups. The essence of education is striking a balance between these two ends. We want the maximum of the general welfare compatible with the blessings of liberty. We want to unleash all possible creative powers in every child which will give the child liberty of expression. But we don't want that type of liberty which leads to anarchy and violence.

The trouble with twentieth-century education everywhere in the world is that it has contributed too much to "pressure group" government inside the nations and "power politics" between the nations. It has tended to emphasize individual smartness at the expense of character. The teaching of character in the schools has seemed to the students both visionary and impractical. Character teaching and emphasis on *general welfare* as supreme over *group welfare* or *individual welfare* must be made exceedingly practical. For they are fundamental to the very life of Western civilization.

Some practical method must be found to teach the values of decency and kindness—to bring the social ideas of the Sermon on the Mount into our daily educational routine. Such education for the children of all lands will determine whether the world is to be one of chaos and war or one of prosperity and peace through co-operation at home and abroad. From any long-run point of view education is, therefore, the most important single activity of civilized man.

This is a shocking statement to make, I know—but the

United States, considering her material wealth, is one of the most backward nations in education in the world. True it is that in certain states we spend 125 dollars of state and local funds a year to educate a child. But in other states the local communities are so poverty-ridden that they find it hard to spend even 25 dollars a year. The poor education received by the children born into these backward areas is both a national disgrace and a national peril. Before the war, state and local governments spent $2,100,000,-000 annually on schools. After the war we should spend a minimum of $3,000,000,000, of which the state and local authorities might furnish $2,700,000,000 and the Federal government $300,000,000. The cost of World War II to the Federal government has averaged around $300,000,000 a day. Surely, it can spend as much in a year to support our public-school system—which, after all, is a front line of defense of our national liberties.

Federal *support* of education, however, must never be allowed to become Federal *control* of education. Here again, as in housing and health, control must rest upon the democratic basis of full co-operation within the community. In fact, the community faces its greatest responsibility in meeting the challenge of education.

In the adult field, too, all of our educational authorities —Federal, state, and local—must be alert to the opportunities for expansion. I am certain that with full postwar employment, we have here an unlimited opportunity of service to our nation and to our society. Newly awakened creative instincts of the adults can be as important for the future peace and development of the world as the education of our children.

None of us is too old to learn something new. It is just a question of wanting to learn with the whole intensity of our being. I put in enough spare time to learn a little Spanish at fifty—a little Russian at fifty-five—and, at fifty-six, enough about flying so I could solo and land a plane by myself. And I have known of others who learned to fly at seventy. Moreover, the older folks, by learning new things, often stimulate their children. I'm sure that if I hadn't learned Spanish, my daughter and one of my sons would never have studied the language.

As a nation, we would have a much broader knowledge of international affairs if more of us learned another language. For if you really learn another language you become acquainted with the music, the literature, the folklore, the history, the living habits—even the business methods—of another people. You have a new source of knowledge and pleasure; you make countless new friends. The United States is entering a new era in world affairs—an era of hitherto unknown greatness and responsibility for the maintenance of peace. All of us can help in the international task ahead of us by absorbing another culture in addition to our own.

Each of us can become fairly expert in something new if we will focus our attention in that one direction day after day. Then we are drawn together with others who have the same kinds of interests—and we learn from each other. My own belief is that, although different teaching techniques may be required, the elders can learn just as easily as the young. And in thus broadening their culture and their perspective, the elders acquire a new sense of appreciation that contributes immeasurably to their attainment of the fuller life.

Surely, in this attainment, both the young and old must stand together against ignorance and darkness. Together, we must devote our spirit and our energy to the highest possible ideal. This is the particular job of applying education to attainment of the religious ideal—the integration of the whole man in the service of the highest order of life.

The Nazis were diabolically successful in using their dark religion to force the integration of the whole man in the service of the lowest order. Theirs was the God of War. Ours is the God of Peace. Their methods were force and terror. Ours must be peaceful persuasion and respect for the innate possibilities in every human soul. The road to war is short. The road to peace is long. It takes infinitely more patience, energy, and time to integrate the whole physical and spiritual drive of man in behalf of good than in behalf of evil. We must strive to integrate all aspects of human living, whether they have to do with politics, family life, artistic appreciation, or religion. Only as we achieve a balanced development of these five aspects of living can we achieve a genuinely full and fruitful life.

This fuller life will not be easy to get and keep, but it will be impossible to get and keep unless we make the fullest use of our manpower and our resources. If we fall short, we will fall short of our destiny as a great and free people.

THE FULLER LIFE AND POLITICS

To realize this destiny of ours, we must reconcile political and economic democracy in the service of the full life. Our political parties must stand for something definite in terms of the general welfare and the fuller life for all. Our elections must determine more precisely just how the people's representatives vote on all the fundamental issues of dominating importance for full employment and peace.

The representatives of the people will work more intelligently and more effectively in behalf of the general welfare *only* if the people, themselves, become more intelligent and more effective as an electorate. Constituents who insist that their representatives place undue emphasis on local and special interests are placing an undue burden on those representatives who earnestly strive to stand for the general welfare as well as for the welfare of their constituents. The level of statesmanship in Congress, therefore, directly reflects the level of political and economic education of the voters—and the level of political activity right on down to the precinct.

In recent years less than 60 per cent of the eligible voters have participated in presidential and congressional elections. If no greater proportion participates in the immediate postwar elections, this would mean that our national policies on employment and peace would be determined by only around 60 million voters. We must have greater participation. While 60 million jobs is a reasonable economic objective for 1950, 60 million voters is far too low a political objective.

Our society has become so complex that the need for more general understanding of the working of the parts and the interdependence of the parts is imperative. It would be extremely healthy, therefore, if the current trends in political-economic education were greatly accelerated in the next decade by more and more doorbell ringing and pamphleteering.

The proposition of political activity is simple. How many eligible voters are there in your precinct? How many voted in the last election? In other words, what is the index of political action in your precinct, your community, your city? I think that the citizens in any community, outside of the poll tax states in the South, should be ashamed if the index of their community fell below 70 per cent.

In a democracy like ours, with its many educational and informational channels, political-economic illiteracy should be as inexcusable as ordinary illiteracy. I believe that every voter should work out his own index of political activity to be used to keep an accounting of himself, his President, his Senators and Representatives, and the openly organized "pressure groups"—as well as those lobbyists and political fixers which the voter can keep in sight in the maze of Washington's "invisible Congress." I would call this system of tabulation the Civic Index of the People's Peace of Full Employment.

The component parts of this Civic Index, of course, would change as the basic national issues changed. On the issue of full employment as set forth in this book, the index would be made up of these ten points of essential action:

1. *Assigning responsibility* to government for preparing and keeping a current accounting of the nation's budget of job and investment opportunities.

2. *Reducing taxes* in a balanced manner so as to stimulate private initiative, to increase consumption, and to protect the public interest against special tax privileges.

3. *Maintaining wages* to protect the take-home pay, and raising minimum wages to provide a minimum standard of living.

4. *Maintaining prices* of farm products to sustain farm income and consumption, and *adjusting industrial prices* to promote consumption.

5. *Promoting resource development* by the use of Federal investment in river-valley authorities, rural electrification, and soil conservation, to build up a backlog of private job opportunities.

6. *Elimination of trade barriers* both internal and external by opposing monopolistic practices whether applied by a foreign cartel, a domestic trust, a trade union, or a farm organization.

7. *Providing a housing program* to assure adequate

214

homes for all groups, to be co-ordinated under a government housing agency.

8. *Extending social security and health insurance* by universal coverage for unemployment and old-age insurance, by universal health insurance and adequate medical facilities, and expanded public-health services.

9. *Promoting educational equality* by Federal grants-in-aid to provide better facilities everywhere.

10. *Guaranteeing security* at home and abroad by fostering conditions that make for racial and religious tolerance and international good will and co-operation.

Making politics a vital part of the fuller life calls for no apologies. Quite definitely to the contrary, I believe that we can earn our fuller life only by devoting a part of our leisure to political discussion and activity. Our free-enterprise democracy can progress only through political parties and politicians, good and bad. It is the people's job to encourage the good politicians and eliminate the bad.

Politics needs the vigor and freshness of our young men and women. Politics offers to them their only opportunity to help shape the world they want for themselves and their own children. The place to begin is the precinct. The time is today and tomorrow and the next day—not just a few days before an election. Only with the full participation of our youth in politics shall we be able to excel other nations not only in the art of political democracy, but also in the science of reconciling our political freedom with the need for full use of all manpower, all resources, and all technologies in behalf of the general welfare. This demands both political education and a co-operative spirit—the same kind of spirit in peace which we have shown in war.

This is both the challenge and the dilemma of democracy—namely, how to get full production, preserve the fundamental freedoms, and then go forward toward objectives which are worthy of man's spirit. In all this there can be no compulsion except that which comes from the earnest search of man's spirit to discover the divine purpose of the universe. Full employment with abundance for all is good; but by itself it is not enough. Peace is good, but not enough. The rights of man are essential; but by themselves, they are not enough. We cannot attain abundance, peace, and freedom without recognizing one thing even more basic. And that one thing is the fatherhood of God and the fundamental decency of man.